Angels Don’t Cry

Angels Don't Cry
Omnec Onec

This publication is the only authorized version from Omnec Onec.

Publisher's Website: ***https://discuspublishing.com***

Cover Design: Peter Holle

Layout: Anja Schäfer

ISBN: 978-3-910804-10-4

Omnec Onec

Angels Don't Cry

Autobiography

Table of Contents

Introduction

We all make mistakes, so that we can learn from them. Likewise, we have to learn to accept our negative parts and problems, to laugh about ourselves, to believe in the positive and good and to focus our whole attention on it. We may never forget that our imagination is the key to creation.

In the first part of my autobiography with the title "From Venus I Came" I have described my life on the astral level on the planet Venus. This now is the personal account and description of my life on Planet Earth – a very strong contrast to my life of peace and beauty on Venus. I had been told by Uncle Odin and Aunt Arena that some Earth people believed Venusians to be angels.

Three years after my arrival, when I was only ten Earth years old, I was chosen to play an angel in the school Christmas play. My grandmother was a Christian and seemed to know a lot about angels and the human concept of heaven. She told I me all she had read about them including the wings and the halo. She seemed amused at my interest. I sat on the floor while she read from the bible where the angels appeared to the shepherds.

When I asked her, "Grandma, do angels cry?" she looked up in surprise and said: "No, I don't believe they do. It seems to be their work to protect people from pain and suffering. So they sort of dry people's tears." – "Grandma", I said, "do you think it is okay for me to be an angel because I do cry?"

She hugged me laughing and replied: "You will always be my angel if you cry or not, because I know you only cry if you have to or for others."

I continued my tearful journey here on Earth, learning about emotions unknown to me such as fear, anger, and aggression. And at the worst times, I always told myself in a whisper: "Angels don't cry, Angels don't cry."

In reading this story of my life, it may seem unreal how one major experience or crisis follows another, day after day. It often seemed to me that I was given a rest only long enough to catch my breath, and yet another crisis would unfold, often leaving my mind reeling and my emotions topsyturvy.

This is what the Masters in Retz on Venus meant when they explained to me, that due to this being my last incarnation in the Physical, to expect a heavy load of Karma because of the choice I made to take Sheila's suffering. I as Soul had created certain conditions which were difficult for my own experiences which would prepare me to my future mission here on Earth. They assured me that good will come from all the bad experiences and that in the future I would understand.

Many years later, I saw that what they explained was true. Many people on Earth have suffered as I have, and because of my suffering, they will be able to relate to me as a human being rather than an alien. Perhaps even inspired to accept and learn better to cope with their own difficulties. We all have our special angels to guide and protect us and even some physically here on Earth, disguised as friends who are there to comfort us and help us dry our tears and heal our wounds.

To all my special angels here – THANK YOU!

Amual Abactu Baraka Bashad
(May the Universal Love and Blessings be)

Omnec Onec

What happened so far

Summary of From Venus I Came – Autobiography Part 1

In the first part of Omnec's life story, "From Venus I Came," the author describes her first years on her home planet of Venus, and more specifically, its astral plane.

After its atmosphere was destroyed thousands of years ago by environmental catastrophes and Venus became uninhabitable, the Venusians crossed over into the astral dimension of being, which may seem to us like a fairy tale land. Within the higher astral plane, the power of thought alone can manifest things out of nothing, and its inhabitants can teleport from one place to another. In addition, the Venusian people usually live many hundreds of years.

Omnec's Venusian mother Shawik-Echo Lei died in childbirth, and her grief-stricken father Deashar was incapable of caring for the child. Deashar placed Omnec into the care of Arena, the sister of his deceased wife, and her husband Odin, with whom the young girl grew up and spent her early, carefree years. In Teutonia, a cultural center on Venus, Omnec made visits to the temples of knowledge, and was initiated by Odin and Arena into the laws of the Supreme Deity.

After her pilgrimage to the city of Retz, a spiritual master explained to young Omnec that she had been chosen by the Council of the Brotherhood of Planets for an important mission. He explained to her that she would take on a physical body, travel to planet Earth, and grow up there in an earthly family. The goal of her mission would be to gain first-hand insight into all shades of Earthly life. Her mission would better enable the Venusians, who had been involved in colonizing Earth aeons ago, to better understand their brothers and sisters of Earth, and thus help them to spiritually improve and transform their society. As well, Omnec's mission would include enlightening Earth's people about their true origins and history, so that they could better mature and eventually be ready to be accepted into the Brotherhood of Planets, an association of spiritually advanced inhabitants of our solar system. In carrying out her mission Omnec would gain the opportunity to dissolve her own karmic entanglements created in her previous incarnations on earth.

The spiritual master explained to Omnec that it was entirely her decision whether or not to accept this assignment. Curious as she was, Omnec chose to enter into this adventure, and her assigned teacher Vonic intensively prepared her for her new life on Earth.

When the time came, Omnec returned to Retz, a city which exists not only on the astral plane, but also under a climatic dome on the physically hot surface of Venus. Retz serves as a gateway into different dimensions, and here young Omnec received a physical body through a modification in her vibration, after which, accompanied by her uncle Odin, she traveled in a large spaceship to Earth.

The Venusian spacecraft landed in a hidden valley in Kashmir. In Agam Des, "the largest spiritual city on planet Earth," she first spent one year in a Tibetan monastery. For centuries, space travelers have landed here to adjust to Earth's coarser vibrations. There, Omnec laboriously learned to move in a physical body, and how to nourish and care for it.

After this year of adjustment, she traveled in a smaller spaceship with her uncle and a companion to the United

States, where they landed in the Nevada desert. A contact awaited them there, and he transported their small group in a car to their destination in Arkansas called Little Rock. Upon their arrival, Odin, Omnec and the companion waited in the bushes for a coach. Inside the coach, a seven-year-old Earth girl named Sheila Gipson was riding from her mother's home to her grandmother in Tennessee, with whom she would be living permanently. The spiritual masters on Venus had foreseen that this bus would have an accident and that little Sheila would die. The spiritual masters also recognized that Omnec was closely connected with Sheila through multiple common past-life incarnations. So it was that Omnec had been prepared by the Venusians to look like Sheila, dress like her on the day of the foreseen event, and to be ready to take young Sheila's place upon her foreordained death.

The accident occurred as foreseen, and unnoticed by the other bus passengers, Omnec was exchanged for the dead Sheila, who, to the earthlings, never appeared to die. On schedule, she arrived in Chattanooga at the grandmother's house, who never recognized the exchange of the two similarily-looking children because she had not seen her grandchild in several years. Having learned from her teacher Vonic all the relevant details about Sheila's life on Venus, such as the names of her closest relatives, and appearing nearly identical to the deceased Sheila, Omnec easily fit into her new family. However, the comparatively primitive life on Earth, and especially the racial prejudices of the Southerners caused her considerable interior suffering.

Despite those circumstances, Omnec, now as Sheila, lived a largely carefree and sheltered life in Tennessee thanks to the loving care of her grandmother. However, she longed to be with her earthly "mother" Donna, to whom she felt an inexplicably strong attraction. Unfortunately, those visits were rare. Donna, who was only fifteen years old when Sheila was born, was leading an unsteady life with a man named C.L. and both were constantly on the move. Finally, Omnec's longing was satisfied when she was invited by Donna to visit her on Sanibel Island in Florida, where she worked with C.L. as the manager of a vacation village.

Chapter 1 – Living with a Dictator

It was a warm June day in 1962 when I climbed aboard the bus bound for Florida. I entered my life here on Earth on a bus and now it was once again one of these grey buses that should take me to my mother. I was excited and looking forward to seeing her again. What would we experience together?

I reflected back as we left the city limits of Chattanooga. My life with my grandmother in Chattanooga was exciting and sometimes disturbing. I learned countless things about life on Earth. Now I was looking forward to new experiences in a different part of the country. It was not the beautiful lush green mountains and scenery that I was glad to leave but the level of consciousness of the area. The limited view of the people caused by their Christian faith and prejudices was very often confusing to me. I remembered one incident in particular:

It was one of the rare cold winters in Chattanooga when we had ice and snow. We had services at the church we went to three times a week. It was a Monday night and we were on our way to prayer meeting. We were walking with a group of people. I was one of the few young children going to these services.

There was a family of black people that lived across the street on the corner from the church. Coming closer we could see smoke and flames, and in the distance was the sound of fire truck sirens approaching. I began to run when I saw that it was the house of the black family that was on fire.

When I got there I could see the lady running out of the house carrying a bundle in her arms and shouting for help. She laid a small child on the snow-covered ground wrapped only in a diaper! She ran back inside to get more of her children or belongings

I have seen all these people standing there, not helping, just watching her panic and the baby crying. I ran into the yard, got onto my knees and picked up the child of about three months old. I opened my coat and put the baby inside and stood up holding it against my body to keep it warm.

Soon grandma was by my side, then we heard voices from the crowd of people: "What do you think you are doing? That is a nigger baby! What are you? A nigger lover?!"

I started to cry: "Grandma, why are they angry at me? We cannot let this little baby freeze and be scared! They are supposed to be Christians!"

Then the black lady came and took the baby out of my arms and I was shuffled off to the church for services.

I remembered many occasions just like this one. It wasn't my grandmother, she had taught me to love and care for people. She never dwelled on race. She had much love and compassion and was gentle and kind to everyone.

She was born to a well-known family. There is even a street named after them. She was married to a man of Irish-English descent who worked at a coal-mine. When he died of the black lung and left her with eleven children and the family lost all their money after the war, she had to go to work. She did housework for a black doctor's family during the depression. This was very unusual at that time and she was always thankful to them.

I would miss her, she was the one who cared and loved me here. She was my protection. I really felt bad about leaving her. Still I was looking forward to seeing more about Earth. I was convinced that people in different areas had to feel differently about life and themselves.

As I looked out the bus window I could see palm trees: Florida – it was very flat and sunny!

When we arrived in Fort Myers, I looked for Donna but didn't see her. Suddenly a tall man in a hat walked over and called "Sheila?" I stood there looking at C.L's smiling face. He was about 6 feet tall, hazel eyes, dark hair and a mustache. My heart sank, I really was hoping she would come. He took my suitcase and I followed him to the car. He scared me.

"Where's Mommy?" I asked timidly. "Oh, she's on the island. We have to take the ferry over," he replied. "A ferry!" I exclaimed. For a moment I forgot my fear. It would be my first boat ride ever.

The ferry trip to Sanibel Island was as lovely and exciting as I imagined. On the horizon was a strip of green, barely visible as I craned my neck over the side. What gorgeous sights greeted us as we docked and began our drive through the lush jungle! Most of the island was a tropical wilderness of palm trees, palmetto grass, skunk cabbage, and oh so many wild-looking plants. Flamingos and wild rabbits seemed to be everywhere. It was paradise.

Leaving the main road, we soon came upon a cluster of cottages set upon wooden stilts. All around were miniature orange bushes. The ocean sounded very close. "This is the Sandcastles Resort", C.L. announced. He stopped the car in a small clearing, just ahead of the resort office.

Seconds later the door burst open and a beautiful woman in shorts ran toward us. Donna! Her long curly blond hair swinging and bouncing. It was all the way to her waist! Her skin was a deep, rich brown, and she looked so full of vigor, so alive. She threw her arms around me, just about squeezed me to death. It was so wonderful to see her again.

She was done with work every day at four, she told me happily. Then she was free to do anything, go swimming in the resort's pool, or perhaps walk the beach collecting shells.

Sanibel Island was famous for the many varieties of sea shells that washed up on the shores.

The beach was fantastic! Sandpipers were running up and down, jumping as the waves came in. All of this, the roar of the sea, the salty crisp breeze, the thousands of purple, yellow, and pink coquina shells looking like butterflies took my thoughts back to Tythania's shores and the times I sat, with buried toes, just staring out to sea. It reminded me of the life I left behind that night we landed in the Nevada desert.

I waded out into the water, splashing with my feet as the waves came in, enjoying the afternoon sun. A beautiful multicolored flower came floating along and I moved to pick it up from underneath. Mom's screams rang in my ears. I froze. She dashed over and grabbed my hand, a look of terror in her eyes. That beautiful floating thing was not a flower – it was a deadly jellyfish!

Mom pointed to the left. What a sight! Hundreds of flamingoes flocked on a distant sandbar. They were just too beautiful for words, like a pink cloud when a whole bunch flew off. Here was the flamingoes' mating place. It was very uncommon, Mom said, to see them like this. They always choose out-of-the-way places to mate.

The sun was beginning to set, and my mother motioned for us to go. "We've got to hurry because the mosquitoes come out, and they're really bad around here."

Our cottage turned out to be way back in the woods. As soon as we drove up, I was warned to run as fast as I could into the house. Otherwise the mosquitoes would eat me alive. I was certain Mom was exaggerating. Sure enough, moments after I got out of the car my arm was black, and I mean black. It was frightening because the air was filled with clouds of them, and they covered my face and all the exposed parts of my body. There was nothing I could do but wipe them off by the handful.

For dinner we ate shrimp boiled in beer. I wasn't sure whether I would like them because I never tasted shrimp, and I surely never heard of boiling them in beer. But I loved them! They tasted like out of this world. Shrimp boiled in beer are among my favorite foods ever since. Going to sleep listening to all the night sounds, all the creatures in the jungle making noises, was a new and strange experience.

The next day, Mom walked over to a large box and called me over to see something. "What is it?" – "It's my art. See, I have been collecting seashells and I make pictures of some and others are rare because they come down the gulf from other countries, these I save."

She showed me a completed picture. She would glue a piece of plywood to the back of a wooden frame, then paint the frame and background black. She would arrange sand glued along the bottom to form a beach scene, then glue seaweed that she dried in different places making plants, then colorful seashells were glued in the place, little coquino shells were arranged like butterflies. They were simply beautiful and many tourists bought them.

She showed me a book on seashells and I learned the name of various shells. I loved to be together with her. We were enjoying making art till C.L. came noisily back – yelling and obviously drunk. We hurriedly put everything away.

One night at full moon we went out to find seashells. That night the tide would go out away from the island, exposing miles of the ocean floor that was usually under water. It was amazing. It was a breathtaking experience and strangely quiet as we walked into the moonlight. All you could hear was Mom and I laughing and talking. Mom and I walked out onto the exposed sand – it was alive with shells, you could feel them wriggling under your feet. We scooped up all we could into our bucket and carried them back.

C.L. had waited in the office drinking, of course. He did not have the enthusiasm for shell gathering and collecting that we had. He was impatient and drunk. "It's about time", he bellowed. "Let's go out of here." Mom said we would clean the shells tomorrow. C.L. had a violent temper and had on occasion hit Mom.

The next morning Mom and I took a water hose and rinsed the sand off the shells over a screen, then put the washed shells into another bucket. Mom explained to me that we had to boil all the shells to retain their sheen and remove the dead sea creatures – they look like snails or crabs. We had some beautiful and rare ones! We also had Sanddollars. These were very popular among the tourists. When they are first caught, Sanddollars are not as white and glossy as tourists see them. They are really brown and funny-looking until soaked alive in bleach. Soaking them alive in bleach – I thought that was horrible. How could people do such a cruel thing.

I was invited to many social events on the island – dances and parties with other young people whose parents managed other places. I was never allowed to go. C.L. was a very possessive man. I was afraid of him and avoided being alone with him. He had tried to force me to drink many times.

I really loved Sanibel Island and found it peaceful and educational. There was so much to see and learn. Once I was swimming out into the ocean and saw two fins coming toward me. I screamed and started swimming frantically toward shore. Mom was there and she was laughing. I was saying "help, it's a shark!" – "No", she said, "calm down, those are dolphins. When I first saw them, I was scared, too." I looked behind me and saw them jumping in and out of the waves. I loved swimming. In no time at all I learned to swim from one end of the pool to the other. Doing ballet under water was more of a challenge, but it was more fun, too. Swimming in the ocean was no fun. The salty water smelled good, but it burned my eyes and tasted terrible. Most of the time I sat on the beach and stared out to sea, thinking about my new life. Being on Sanibel Island, I appreciated my life on Earth more and more.

As the days passed, my mother and I grew to be close friends. Before, when she visited me in Tennessee, I saw her only two or three days at a time. Now I was with her every day. I could easily have stayed on Sanibel Island for the rest of my life. I wrote Grandma and all the folks back home how wonderful it was.

Even though C.L. wouldn't let me go to the parties, I had plenty of friends. I met and played with the children who came to the resort with their parents.

But as the weeks went by, C.L. became less and less kind. Mom and he were on the road to their old ways again, drinking and fighting. They told me I wasn't going back home to my grandmother. Then Mom and C.L. had a big argument about my going back to school in the fall. C.L. won. He wasn't "going to pay for no brat to go to school."

I wrote Grandma about all this. Her answer was not what I expected: "I won't force you to come back, Sheila, because I know how much you love your mother, even though I have custody of you until you're eighteen." And that was that!

We stayed on Sanibel until mid-August. It was near my 15th birthday when I found out we were leaving, it was a sudden decision of C.L. based on the fact that a lot of money had come in for reservations for fall. C.L. was tempted by all the money and instead of depositing it as he usually did he kept it. Everything valuable he stole. I watched in amazement as C.L. crammed the car full of coins and pop from the vending machines, a typewriter and the two-way marine radio, all of the cash from reservations and payments, and assorted goodies. Now I saw for myself how C.L. did his dirty work. I was shocked, there was no warning, just pack and let's go!

I ran down to the beach. There was a beautiful sunset. This is how I want to remember this beautiful place I thought.

Because there had been talk of a bridge being built from Fort Myers to Sanibel – then I knew big hotels, paved roads and lots of changes would make this a popular rather than a quiet close to nature island.

I heard Mom calling me and turned away from my last glimpse of paradise and all the beautiful living things. I had grown to love these past three months. I sadly walked back to where the car was parked – it was packed full. I had to ride in the front with Mom and C.L. Fortunately they had also packed our trunk full of shells. It was getting dark as we headed for the cottage to get our clothes and to wait for daylight and the first ferry. C.L. wanted to be across the state line as soon as possible since he was stealing everything he could. He said we were going to Mexico. It was the 15th of August and as I rode miles down the road. I thought, where will I be in five days on my birthday? I wished I had known we were leaving, then I could have written Grandma or called her. Even though my life with her had been boring it had been secure. By all means I had to try to keep in touch with her. So here I am, starting a new episode in my life. First Mom showed me how to mix drinks. She was sitting between me and C.L. who was speeding as always. The vodka was on the floor on my side of the car with some lime and grapefruit soda. I liked the soda but not the vodka.

Well, here I am mixing drinks as we drive down a highway toward Mexico. What a life! It certainly wasn't boring.

I closed my eyes to reflect on the place we had just left, the only place close to paradise on Earth since I left Venus. But even Sanibel could not compare with it. Life on Venus seemed only a beautiful dream.

I always wanted to remember Sanibel Island with its soft white warm sand, palm trees waving in the warm balmy wind. The sound of the ocean, peaceful yet powerful. The jungle foliage in the background. The sandpipers chasing the waves – running out and in with them. Sometimes dolphins' cries mixed with seagulls'. The hot sun – softly warming the body and turning it golden brown. How the moon made a silver path across the ocean that I dreamed of dancing on in my astral or Soul body. The sun rises turning the water pink and gold.

Even storms were wonderful – the ocean becoming dark blue and grey. How you could see the rain in the distance as it approached your area. Falling in blue grey swirls from the dark thunder clouds toward the earth. Thunder rolling off, then becoming louder, lightning playing across the heavens, creating a special-effect for those who watched! Raindrops falling back into the ocean from were it came. Each drop making small circles running into one another, almost looking like drops of silver and jewels from above. The wind which had increased made the water look rough and foreboding.

I loved the calmness, as the dark clouds blew away and the sun once again dominated the sky over the island, color once again becoming aquamarine blue. Water dripping off the trees sparkling like so many jewels decorating the plants. How quickly the sand absorbed the moisture as once again everything took on a certain clearness. The rain had washed away the dust and haze, returning my paradise to new beauty and wonder…

I was jolted back to reality by the halting of the car! We had arrived in Mexico. Only a few days later we went back to Florida. We rented a bungalow just across the backyard from C.L.'s mother. None of C.L.'s family really cared for him. Leslie, C.L.'s daughter, couldn't stand him. She mentioned to Mom that she didn't trust C.L. around her four little girls, and most of the family knew that Leslie's mother lost a child because of C.L.'s beatings.

I began to see more and more of the mean side of C.L. Why he had such a terrible temper I didn't know; but I remembered that his own mother believed he was possessed by a demon.

C.L. was a dictator, a very domineering person. I was afraid of him, always nervous in his presence. Everything had to be done his way, and violence was his favorite sport. If Mom and I didn't eat when he wanted us to, and what he wanted us to, he would hit the both of us. If the food wasn't cooked the way he liked it, regardless of what we liked, C.L. would be furious. When I asked for ketchup for a hotdog, C.L. screamed: "I don't eat ketchup on my hotdog, nobody else eats ketchup on their hotdogs ... only a fool eats ketchup on their hotdog!" On another occasion, Mom got up from the table to go to the washroom,

C.L. promptly beat her on the head for not asking permission.

So there were many days when Mom and I sat on the porch hoping C.L. wouldn't come home. Later, when we lived out West and C.L. was in the contracting business, we hoped he would fall off a scaffold and break his neck. That's how bad it was to have him around.

C.L. hated music, except of course when he himself was singing. And he hated radios, too. Mom and I enjoyed sitting up at night, talking and listening to country western music. Usually he went to bed early and was sound asleep before we dared turn it on. But for C.L., quiet was not quiet enough. "Shut the God-damned radio off!" his voice would boom from the bedroom. Living with C.L. was like being in a prisoner-of-war camp. In ways it was worse.

Uncle Odin once said that a person who doesn't like music is certainly being controlled by the negative forces. C.L. had no interests in culture. His only loves were money and liquor.

Logic was one gift C.L. had more than enough of. Because he could make me understand his way of thinking if he had to beat it into me, I learned a great deal from him. I learned how to be logical and practical whenever I needed to be that way.

C.L. punished himself for the loss of his child. He raved about how he had beaten his wife, his pregnant wife, and that the baby was later born without a kidney. Yes, C.L. was mean. But he did have a mental problem and a drinking problem. There were times when he did show his nicer side, but his mood changed drastically from one moment to the next. I could never tell how he would treat us, whether he would be nasty or kind.

C.L.'s bad health came from his drinking, especially the liver sores on his hands. And there was always a newspaper on or near his bed for him to spit on.

I felt sorry for the man as much as I disliked him. C.L. was himself suffering inside, for all the mean things he had done in life. I knew he felt guilty about many many things, and I am sure they will haunt him for a long time to come.

One day, C.L. declared that it was time to do conventional work again, and his new job was at his brother-in-law's produce company. I wasn't sure what he had in mind when he brought home a huge barrel of crushed and moldy fruit. The next day, when there were more grapes, bananas, and oranges, I knew: C.L. was going into the moon-shining business, and Mom and I were his first two (unpaid) employees.

We spent our days slashing and stamping around in a huge foot tub in the living room, squishing the grapes, bananas, oranges, and who knows what else with our bare feet. I can't say we didn't have a hilarious time, Mom and I, dancing around and laughing, and feeling the grapes popping between our toes.

Every day C.L. came home with more fruit, and five pound bags of sugar. Our first problem was with the neighbors; they kept getting a sniff of our fruit. The barrel sat covered with a sheet on the back porch. They assumed we were making preserves, and C.L. readily agreed. The day C.L.'s mother visited us and sniffed her way to the back porch, I could see he was worried. But she too was naive enough to believe the fruit-canning story.

Our wine turned out delicious! One whole day Mom and I sat out on the porch straining the brew into gallon jugs. We carefully lined the funnel with a cloth and poured the well-fermented goop through. Then we had to squeeze the cloth, together with the squishy fruit inside.

C.L. came home and was pleased with our accomplishments. The next day he sold the wine to his fellow workers at the produce company, and this went on for some time. C.L.'s next idea was to drive around the town picking up cases of empty bottles from the bars. Soon we had a whole business going, of Mom and I sitting all day straining the stuff into all sorts of little bottles, and C.L. going out to collect the money. It was full-fledged boot-legging.

Not satisfied with his scope of operations, C.L. began selling by the case. Late at night C.L. would set a case or two out by the mailbox. Early in the morning one of C.L.'s select customers would arrive with the money, stuff it in the mailbox, and pick up a case.

The straining kept us busy for hours and hours, day after day. Never once did we finish our work sober, because of the fumes, and one day it was so bad we couldn't even talk straight. Just then the landlady stopped by to say hello. By the time C.L. came home, Mom and the landlady were stretched out on the living room floor. C.L. laughed. But when the landlady went home, C.L. unleashed his fury. Mom went to bed with yet another beating behind her.

Our business ended as abruptly as it began. The Tampa police somehow got wind of it and came cruising by one day early in the morning. Peeping out the front window we saw the squad car slowing down right by the mailbox, where our case of wine was sitting.

We were terrified! As soon as they were out of sight, C.L. ran out, grabbed that case, and dashed into the backyard. Minutes later we were busy digging a hole. In went the last of our brew from the barrels, and all of the wine Mom and I spent so much time straining. There was so much wine in the hole that the dirt was just floating on top. And did it smell! For days the fumes were like a cloud in our backyard. Willie the Worm, our landlord's sausage dog almost drowned in that hole. The poor little thing waddled around our yard drunk for days.

Shortly afterwards, new difficulties in my life with my mother and C.L. emerged. C.L.'s father came to live with us a few weeks later. That was when all the trouble started. Pap, as we called him, was a nasty old fellow when he drank, and he had a habit of taking all his clothes off and flinging himself across the bed. Mom usually tiptoed in to shut the door. But then there were times when he tried to grab me or feel me, and I complained to her about it. "Well, he's old," she said. "Just ignore him." That's what I did – I stayed away from him.

What I didn't know was that Pap took revenge on me for avoiding him. He gave my mother an earful of lies about seeing me and C.L. together when she was away. Mom never said anything about it, except when she was drunk. Then she and C.L. got into heated arguments about me, while Pap just sat back and laughed.

When she wasn't coming right out and accusing us of sleeping together, she sat around throwing out slurring remarks. C.L. took full advantage of the situation. When Mom was at work he would say: "If we're going to be accused of it, we might as well go ahead and do it."

"Never!" I would reply, ready to break out in tears. Mostly I tried to ignore him.

I was caught in a vicious circle of C.L.'s father trying to make passes and telling my mother lies, my mother accusing

C.L. and me of it, and C.L. himself trying to get me in bed with him.

My stomach turned into knots whenever they took to the bottles. Before long they would be fighting again. I knew this and cried. "Silly little girl," they said, laughing. I couldn't understand how these people could be so mean. It was bad enough to have someone like C.L. around, but Mom's cruelty broke my heart. I had no idea of where to turn for help.

I didn't really blame her. She was being confused by Pap's lies and her knowing about C.L.'s reputation with young girls. And when she was drunk, she said things she normally wouldn't have said.

I became a confused and upset child. I had very little freedom at home, and no friends. In the evenings I loved to sneak out in my bathing suit and run through our neighbor's lawn sprinklers. But it wasn't possible unless everyone at home was drunk. With so little love and affection at home, I was hungry for attention and freedom.

Night after night I looked up into the sky, hoping to see a ship. And I tried to communicate mentally, but nothing came of it. I guess they were reluctant to contact me because then they would have been tempted to help me. But whenever encouraging thoughts entered my mind which I knew weren't my own, I realized how aware they were of what was happening. Thanks to their inner guidance I did not give up, and much of what I would have learned in school came to me in the same way.

Memories of my home in Teutonia, and Odin and Arena, all the beautiful people I once knew, came back to haunt me often. Alone and unhappy, I thought long and hard about all I had given up in exchange for what I was getting. To convince myself again that I needed to accept my life as Karma, and live it out, was harder and harder as the days and weeks dragged on.

I felt trapped and thought of my uncle's words, that "though you suffer, try to see the valuable lessons in these unfortunate experiences." And I remembered my teacher Rami Nuri saying: "All these unhappy moments will bring you many valuable experiences from which you may begin to understand your fellow man and his attitudes."

But these thoughts uplifted me only for a little while. Sitting alone and crying became a way of life the more I realized how terrible my plight was. And this was only a small beginning ...

In time, C.L. again had the urge to move on, to make or take money somewhere else. Virginia was our next stop. Here Mom and C.L. managed "The Barbecue Pit", a truck-stop restaurant. C.L. was great at making barbecue sauce, and had the brilliant idea of building an open pit out in front of the place. To attract customers, he cooked onions on the pit, sending the strong aroma far and wide. We didn't stay in Virginia long enough for any of us to settle down. C.L. had the itch to move on again.

Tired and road weary after a cross-country trip, we climbed out of the car in San Diego, California. A milk truck driver stopped to give us directions, and by the time C.L. was finished with his sob story, the man left us several gallons of milk. He directed us to where the apartments were cheap.

Mom immediately went looking for a waitressing job. Luck was with her. Out on an island in San Diego Bay she was given a well-paying banquet-only position. I enjoyed going to pick her up every day, crossing by ferry and seeing all the night lights of the city.

Meanwhile, C.L. was busy in the contracting business. His work was very simple; he gave free estimates and then arranged for subcontractors to do the job. As soon as a contract was signed, C.L. pocketed the cash. The unsuspecting customers saw the last of him.

One of C.L.'s clients was his dentist. In return for C.L. erecting an addition to the medical offices, the dentist agreed to pay 1000 $, pull all of C.L.'s teeth, and then fit him with false teeth. It was a terrible experience for C.L. to go through. Talk about him being a devil, when he was having his teeth pulled we went through hell with him. Mom and I began to feel like basketballs – we were slapped around so much.

Needless to say, construction on the dentist's building never began. With 1000 $ in his pocket and a new set of teeth, C.L. took off.

But this time luck was against him. Mom and I were still rushing around, packing, when the radios started blaring his description all over San Diego. On a previous visit to San Diego, C.L. had gotten involved with a young girl and finished her off when she got pregnant. Authorities in Texas believed he brought her there before she disappeared.

We did not get far down the highway before a police car pulled us to the side. Mom and I sat in the car, watching, and hoping C.L. would be arrested and taken away. Then we heard the police radio giving out C.L.'s description and license number, while he and the policeman stood outside talking and laughing, and acting like old friends. C.L. had quite a way with people!

C.L. also had a wealth of ideas on how to make money without working. Our hair-raising escape from San Diego did not seem to frighten him in the least. At El Paso we crossed over into Mexico long enough to load up the truck with Tequila and whiskey which he sold for higher prices in the States. Together with C.L.'s savings from his "work" in San Diego, we were able to live for a while in a motel in Phoenix, Arizona. C.L. relaxed at home while Mom worked as a waitress. Then we settled down in a trailer park and C.L. did some more "contracting work".

One night, I heard Uncle Odin calling me. I woke up, it was about 11.30 at night. Mom and C.L. were fast asleep after some heavy drinking. I had gone to bed early to escape. Uncle Odin explained to me that the Brotherhood had decided for me to have a special examination to see what physical and emotional changes were occurring during my life here on Earth.

"How?" I asked. "We are taking care of everything, you only need to get dressed and someone will pick you up at the entrance to the trailer park." "What if they wake up and find me gone?" – "We are using our energy to keep them asleep. Don't worry. We will keep them sleeping till you return." "You mean I am really going to see you again!" I all of a sudden felt a surge of excitement. "Yes, my little one! However, you must calm yourself. I recommend a meditation beforehand. So I can be with you without becoming distressed!"

I did my meditation, got dressed and went to the street to wait. It was very quiet. We were on the outskirts of Phoenix close to the desert. I only saw a few lights as I stood there.

Suddenly a big Cadillac pulled up, the window went down and there was Uncle Odin for the first time since we parted years before! I felt tears – not sad but joy – for the first time I knew tears of joy! There was his handsome loving face that I had missed so much! He stepped out and embraced me. I sobbed. "Don't cry, angel", he said. "I know it has been a terrible ordeal. I wish it could be otherwise, but we have no control over destiny, and you have not only taken on Sheila's Karma but are also paying your own personal debts. I admire your courage for I don't think I could withstand the pain – physical and emotional – that you are experiencing."

I got into the car and he passed me a glass vial with a serum to relax me and for cleansing the negative energy around me so that he could be close to me without an adverse effect on him, Odin explained. "You have been exposed to so much for one so new here." I drank it and felt a strange peace overcome me – not just physical but deeper.

We drove for about 30 minutes and turned off the main road heading into the desert. It was very dark and quiet. We parked and as Uncle Odin helped me out I saw the outline of a spaceship, approx. 30 feet in diameter. It looked like a shadow except for the faintly glowing port holes. There was a small ramp entering the ship's interior. When we arrived inside, I heard a faint humming sound and there was a slight light of bluish tint all around. We were in a circle of a room with two seats in front of a panel with switches and a screen. There were two men waiting for us. I followed them down a very narrow corridor to a small pieshaped room. There was a small table, just like the examining table in a doctor's office. I was asked to take off my clothes. A strikingly handsome man resembling a mixture of Asian and white, obviously a Martian, took them and put them on a small chair. I felt a twinge of self-consciousness because I was alone with three men. This was also something I had learned from living on Earth: to hide your nude physical body from one another.

I lay on the table and a square box was lowered over my body. It had a big crystal in the center much like an eye. It glowed pink and purple and scanned me from top to toe. I felt the warm energy emitting from it – it was very relaxing. I drifted off to sleep. Suddenly Uncle Odin was calling me. I opened my eyes, not sure if I had been dreaming. No, I was still inside the spaceship and Uncle Odin was standing next to me, smiling.

I got up, dressed and went outside to the waiting car. I felt much better than when I arrived, sort of recharged. On the drive back I asked the time, only one and a half hour had passed! I was tired but felt peaceful and reassured that my people still cared and had not abandoned me.

Uncle Odin spoke, receiving my thoughts. "You must never think we don't care for you, you are important to us.

Much depends on what you learn and experience. We are so sad because we can only stand by and watch. But we try to send you protection and love energy to encourage you."

"Yes" I said. "I feel it. I know I must succeed. I chose this as difficult as it is."

I felt comforted when they left me at the entrance of the trailer park. Uncle Odin hugged me and kissed my forehead. "Aunt Arena said to give you a kiss from her. She is still there in our own dimension. She cannot allow herself to join us. Your father is well and he loves you and is proud of you in his own distant way."

I walked back to our trailer, once again to face a different reality – one in which fear and pain were dominating. How long can I protect myself and my Mom, I thought. Nobody had noticed my absence.

For a while, I was content with our life at the trailer park. On many days C.L. came home and tossed bundles of cash on the bed, of tens, twenties, even hundreds. Mom and I had the job of counting the day's pay. We never did figure out how C.L. was able to hoodwink so many people.

As soon as Mom and I began feeling at home and accustomed to our new surroundings, the inevitable happened. C.L. decided to leave Arizona. Two days later we arrived in Albuquerque, New Mexico.

By now it was time that I started my working career, C.L. announced. He wasn't able to find the kind of work he wanted, so he applied for welfare. I of course was nervous, being barely fifteen and not really having a conception of working for a living. With Mom and C.L.'s help, I found a job as a costumed curb girl at a drive-in restaurant. My hours were from twelve midnight until six in the morning. I didn't mind working at night. It was a good feeling to be away from the house for awhile and meet all kinds of people. For someone who had been cooped up for two years it was a relief.

Almost every day a Mexican boy – his name was Miguel – came in to say hello. And he would run up and grab me around my waist, swinging me around. “Hey, you can’t do that in a restaurant!” I’d exclaim. Miguel just laughed. He was crazy about me, and I loved him too. It was my first real romance, my first love in my Earth life.

There were times when Miguel brought me home, and being an outgoing person he naturally wanted to go inside to meet C.L. and Mom. But I knew all too well of C.L.’s racial prejudice. Worse yet, C.L. didn’t even know a boy was driving me home. After I told Miguel about the kind of man C.L. was, he asked if I would run off with him, but as bad as my home life was, I didn’t have the guts to leave home just then. I was too afraid of C.L.

C.L. stunned me one morning. “I’ll pick you up at the restaurant and I don’t want you to leave the place until I get there,” he said. Whether or not he knew what he was doing, he made sure Miguel and I would spend as little time as possible together.

Then one fine morning I waited ... and I waited. One hour, two hours, three – it was ten o’clock and the boss was wondering what I was doing there. I took a cab home. As I stepped inside the door, I could hear C.L. moving about. I sensed trouble ahead. Ignoring him I went into the bathroom to run a bath and sat down at the edge of the tub. C.L. walked in, looking like a devil. “Where have you been all morning?” “What do you mean?” I asked. I was the one who should have been upset. “You told me to wait for you, and I have been waiting till ten o’clock and you didn’t show up.”

“You fucking liar!” he shrilled. “You’ve been whoring around all night, that’s all!” With that C.L. smacked me backwards into the bathtub. My head was sore for days. After that morning I had to be home on time whether he showed up or not. If he was drunk and forgot about me, I was supposed to take a cab home.

A few weeks later, I came home one morning to find us all packed up and ready to leave. C.L. wanted to go to Las Vegas; and that was that. I was heartbroken. I wouldn't even be able to say goodbye to Miguel, couldn't quit my job and pick up my pay. And I couldn't say anything about it because C.L. didn't know I had a boyfriend, and was always accusing me of whoring around. Job or no job, I realized that I was not allowed to have friends of my own, boy or girl. I cried all the way through the desert.

I was really fascinated by the deserts of Arizona and their strange beauty – even though it was a bit barren. There were cactus and beautiful mountains without trees. Then I saw what seemed to be small caves built in the side of cliffs. "What are those?" I asked. Mom explained to me it was Indian dwellings. Here the Indians did not live in tee-pees but in the cliffs, carving out dwellings for themselves and making ladders to climb into them. We stopped at an Indian reservation to look at the goods on sale. They were famous for handmade turquoise jewelry. Most of the Indians were Navajo, but there were some Hopis also. I was more interested in their dwellings and the paintings on the rocks than the jewelry for I knew that these paintings told of their history – I wish I could read and understand them.

I found a large rock that looked as if fires had been set on top of it and climbed up to sit down. It seemed that out of nowhere an old Indian man appeared. I shielded my face from the sun to get a better look at him. Just then an eagle flew over and screamed. How eerie I thought, just like in a strange movie. "Hello", I said timidly. I really did not know if he understood English. He only nodded at me, and then he sat beside me. I noticed that he wore suede clothing: pants and a loin cloth hanging over from the waist, with a beautiful beaded belt of blue-white and red. It seemed to be spiders and the background was black beads. His head band matched with three feathers – white-blue and black and white hanging by a leather thong down his back. His hair was steel grey and almost to his waist parted in the middle, his face very much lined with age and weather. His eyes were kind and sparkling golden brown. He had a slightly crooked nose. He smelled like leather, earth and trees. He smiled at me showing large even white teeth.

"I feel great spirit all around you", he said. All I could say was "thank you." – "You will do much work here, you were sent by the greatfathers of man." He paused. "Your path is difficult but make you strong!" I noticed he gestured with his hands as he spoke, much like we do on Venus!

"You will guide many to understand the Great Spirit that connects all people. It is an honor to be in your presence! Prophecies foretold of your coming. You are the great white hope of future." – "Me?" I gasped. "Don't question fate! Accept that which is to be. Stay strong in spirit always. You are blessed." Thus he stood up, I stood also. "It was so nice to meet you. I am Sheila, I mean Omnec", I blurted out. He took my small hand in his weathered hand. "I am known by many names. One is Chief Nawa Laki." He laid in my palm a ring made of silver, with a small red bloodstone and a larger turquoise one – a symbol he said of the Hopi Spider Clan.

I watched as he walked away. Wow, a real chief! One thing was for sure, it was no dream for I had the gift, my ring! I can't believe I told him my real name, I thought as I headed back toward the tents where all the Indian handcrafts were being sold. I told nobody about this and put the ring in a safe place in my suitcase.

Before we had left, C.L. traded his car for an old 1949 Ford. I hated it; I felt ridiculous in this car because it was so old and we sat so high in our seats. By the time we entered Nevada we had practically overhauled it, and most of our money was gone. Every few hours it broke down. We kept fixing this and fixing that.

Because of C.L.'s liver sores, I ended up doing most of the repairs. I took out and replaced the brake shoes, the gas pump, the oil filter, and other things I've never heard of. I was becoming quite a good mechanic.

In Arizona, not too far from Flagstaff, we cooked our meal over an open fire at a rest stop. C.L., with hacksaw in hand, was trying to fix something on the car.

All day he and Mom had been drinking and arguing, and my nerves were shot, but when I saw C.L. beating her head with this saw, I lost all control. I scrambled up the boulders and hills screaming and crying that I wasn't coming down. Not until they stopped fighting. I just couldn't stand it any longer. C.L. and Mom, drunk as they were, begged and pleaded with me to come down. They would never fight again. Promise! I knew it would only be for the time being. But I was happy to see Mom wasn't really hurt.

A few miles from Boulder Dam the old Ford died. There we sat, in the scorching desert heat, while C.L. walked to the dam for help. He returned with water for the radiator, but it was no use. After an unbearably long wait a good man stopped his car to see what our trouble was. He pushed us the rest of the way to the dam and across.

I loved Boulder Dam. It was so enormous, so amazing and majestic. The huge, sheer rock wall to each side fascinated me. And I relished the desert, the wide open spaces, the quiet at night, the colorful desert plants. Most of all I loved the everblue skies and dry heat of daytime. I felt closer to my people here than anywhere else. This was the beautiful state of Nevada I had first seen on coming to the United States. Nearby, somewhere out there in the wilderness, my uncle had landed our ship on that memorable night almost nine years ago. With that realization all of the beautiful memories of my real home came back to me. "Thank you, Supreme Deity," I whispered. I sat there, watching for spaceships, hoping one of them would land. I wondered, with tears in my eyes, if my life ever would get any better. I felt lonely and forsaken, confused and depressed.

We coasted down the highway toward Boulder City. Somewhere on the road our car conked out. C.L. was trying to decide what our next move would be. He was busy blaming everything on Mom, including our car breaking down. His logic was beyond me. I was just a big knot of nerves. Everything was always someone else's fault. And if I didn't agree I was guilty, then he would smack me until I did.

As the sun began sinking to the horizon our thoughts turned to worries. Where would we spend the night? What would we eat for breakfast in the morning? And for dinner?

Just then a pickup truck slowed down and pulled over. "Need some help?" A huge fellow with a cheery expression stepped down – George Fishman was his name. For hours he and C.L. worked on that car without break until they both knew it was no use. But by then C.L. had made it very clear how desperate we were, and George invited us to his home for dinner.

The Fishmans lived on the outskirts of Boulder City. From their backyard we could see Lake Mead, with its impressive peaks jutting out in the middle. C.L. felt right at home with them. George's father and C.L. struck up an immediate friendship, with C.L. doing most of the talking. I could tell that his con talk was in high gear. I felt very uneasy.

C.L.'s scheme was to start a chain link fence business, which very few people were involved in. It was actually a very good business idea here in Nevada.

We lived with the Fishmans for several weeks, during which time the old man spent 6000 $ putting C.L. in business. That included a brand new four-wheel-drive pickup truck. I liked George's father very much; the whole family was so warm and kind. I dreaded the thought of C.L. someday running off with the goods, but there was little I could do.

I was amazed and delighted to see Mom and C.L. so peaceful together, so happy. But it didn't take me long to realize it was only a front for the Fishmans, as far as C.L. was concerned. And instead of getting better, or even staying the same, times got worse.

C.L. was doing very well in the fence business. For a while he was also doing welding, because it was a quick way to make money, and C.L. loved money. The trouble was that he was having a hard time with his liver. Raw, open sores appeared on his hands. I wasn't surprised to see it happen – every day he and Mom drove fifteen miles to buy liquor because Boulder City was a dry town.

C.L. was a devil when he was well, but he was twice as mean when he was sick. He never ran out of trivialities to yell about. Mom and I were more like servants than family.

I didn't have friends because I never got out of his sight, except when I was working. When I went to the store I was timid, and if I wasn't back in five minutes, not matter how busy the store was, I was spanked. That's the way it was – I was constantly terrified.

When Mom and I heard of two openings for nurses aides at Boulder City Hospital, and the good pay, our waitressing jobs fell by the wayside. Even though we had to give bed baths and enemas, and change the bed pans, we loved our new jobs. What counted most was that we were away from C.L. all day. Our day began by going into the rooms to record pulses, blood pressures, and temperatures. We served meals, and made the beds, and did whatever the nurses asked us to do.

I will never forget the day one of the nurses cornered me and told me to do an enema. We had all been trained how to do an enema, but this was my first time. She pointed to a door. Bravely as I could, I entered the room, shaking. Then I saw her, and nearly dropped dead with fright! She must have weighed 500 pounds! Oooh dear. Never in my life did I see such a fat lady, and here I was the one to give her an enema. I was afraid because at 15 years I weighed 89 pounds, and since I was so skinny, most heavy people seemed to dislike me. I understood that either they had gland problems or were naturally big just as I was small. I always felt sorry for the ones with health problems.

She was lying with her back to me in an open gown, so I marched up and acted as if I did this every day. I pushed the tube between her fleshy buttocks. The tube went in, and in, and in. I kept pushing but nothing happened. "What the hell is going on?" I wondered. "This stuff isn't emptying out like it should". The pressure inside the body was supposed to do the work. I decided to take a peak and spread the fold apart. Oh, no! My stomach seemed to turn inside out. The tube had gone round and round inside a wrinkle. By the time I did it right, I was so upset and embarrassed that I spilled the stuff all over the lady's back and myself. The lady was nice about it – she roared with laughter, but I ran out. From then on I hid in the broom closet whenever it was time for enemas.

Next I learned how to give a prep. I had never seen it done before, so fortunately a nurse was going to show me how. At the last moment she was called out. My patient was an old lady who was about to have a hysterectomy. I made my approach with the razor and bowl of water which the nurse had handed me. "But how am I going to do this without soap?" I wondered. Into the bathroom I went to lather up, came back and went to work. Somehow it wasn't working out. The old woman started bouncing on the bed, calling for help, and trying to reach the buzzer. This was disturbing; I never experienced such behavior in my whole life. A nurse came running in and shooed me out. The poor woman was going into hysterics.

"What on Earth were you doing?" the nurse asked when she came out of the room. "I was rubbing soap on her with my hands. You can't shave someone without soap", I answered. She broke out laughing. "Sheila, don't you know you don't put soap on them? You can't rub people like that down there! She thought you were queer." "Well, what does that mean?" I really did not know what queer meant. After she had explained, I was so embarrassed that I never went into that room again. And the lady gave strict orders for me to stay out.

The next escapade got us both into trouble – Mom and I. In fact, we were close to being out of a job. She and I were arguing about who was going to kill the spider on the wall; we were deadly afraid of spiders. Mother finally gave in, got up on a chair, and threw her shoe. Not only did she almost break her neck trying to get away, but her shoe landed on the patient's broken leg. Our faces turned red, he screamed bloody murder, and the spider got away! Every time we went into that room again, not only did we get mean looks from the old man, but we were afraid that the spider might still be there waylaying us.

C.L.'s bad temper was still haunting us, but he was not drinking as much because he was putting on a show for the lawyers. C.L. had had a hernia for a long time but only recently saw a chance to have the operation paid for by insurance. The site at which he was welding had an electrical short, and the lights would go out every time a truck passed. C.L. pretended to trip and fall once when the lights were out.

Up to this time C.L. had been quieter than usual. C.L. and Mom got drunk less often, which was still pretty bad. Again and again when she was drunk, she hammered away at me about sleeping with C.L. And C.L. hammered away at me about actually doing it. I cried. C.L. started making passes, and I hated it, but there was nothing I could do except try to ignore him. I surely could not say anything to Mom. She was the one who was accusing me in the first place. When I was not crying about something that C.L. was doing, I cried about something C.L. had done. In fact, I cried all the time, about so many, many things. But the worst was still to come.

Every morning I had to bring C.L. his coffee and newspaper in bed because he was sick, he claimed. On this particular day, the one I will never be able to forget, I delivered his paper and coffee and went back to bed as usual. My bedroom was just across the hall.

"Sheila!" he called.

"What do you want?"

"Come in here!" he yelled.

"I already gave you your coffee and paper and I want to go to sleep", I called back.

"Get in here, damn it!" his voice roared. A moment passed. "If you don't get in here I'll drag you by your hair!"

My fear was mounting. Donna was out working at the hospital. C.L. was the kind of man who would pull me by my hair. I stepped inside his door to see C.L. glaring at me. "Now what did I do wrong?" I thought.

"Get in this bed with me", he said vehemently.

"No!"

"God damn it, get in here!" he shrilled.

"I won't, C.L., I won't!" I cried.

For a moment I was too stunned to move.

I never expected to see such a sick man jump up so fast to grab me. Face to face with the brute I did not have a chance to do much struggling and kicking. My resisting only made C.L. more furious. He tore my pajamas with one hand and slammed his fist into my head so fiercely that I thought he would kill me.

I lay there limply while C.L. went through the motions.

He hurt me, hurt me badly, as I cried and cried and could not stop. All of my emotions, of horror and shame and fear, seemed to flow out at once. I closed my eyes, squeezed them shut, hoping it all was just a nightmare.

C.L. didn't say a word, just got up and went to the bathroom. I ran to my room and buried my head in the pillow, sobbing. He did not care how I felt, that he had so hurt me and used me. In my spasms of crying, all my feelings of how I loathed this man came out. Then I heard C.L.'s voice:

"If you tell your mother, I'll say that you let me do it, that you led me on. She'll hate you for it. You know she'll never believe you".

For hours I cried, until my eyes ran dry and I fell asleep exhausted. I wanted so badly to tell Mom when she came home, yet I was terrified of what she would say if I told her. And what if C.L. himself told her – she would believe him. I shuddered. Two years was a long time for someone to continue accusing me of sleeping with C.L.

There was no one to turn to or talk to. I realized that people would believe it was all my fault, as they do to this day when I recall the story to them. The reason I had for not telling anyone was fear of being rejected and badly judged.

In the days that followed, C.L. began to offer me drinks. I accepted them eagerly, one after another as a way of escape, to forget and blank out what was happening. "Let's go out to the desert", he would suggest practically every day, and I knew what he had in mind. But most of the time I was too drunk to remember anything. At nights I cried. I was going through so much pain and I just could not tell my mother.

I appealed to my people. "Why don't you help me? Don't let me suffer any more." They answered – I had no choice but to go through with this. For a long time, I could not understand them. I felt they were being cruel to me, had forsaken me. I watched their ships in the nighttime sky, and listened to their messages: I must have strength and realize that I have to pay for what I had done in the past. C.L. was a sick man, in turmoil too, and I should feel sorry for him. As Soul he knew he was doing wrong, but stood by helplessly while his mind and body were possessed and out of control.

I noticed when he was violent his eyes, usually grey, became a yellowish green. However, he would beg me to read to him from the bible and it would calm him. Sometimes he would cry and say he did not know why he was so aggressive or speak guiltily of things he had done that hurt others.

Afterwards, I was reminded of a story C.L.'s mother had told me. During the depression, when C.L. was about three years old, they were living in an old train boxcar, not having a lot of money. One night, there was a terrible thunderstorm and much lightning. The lights went out for only a moment or two, when C.L. who was sleeping in his bed let out a horrible scream which terrified her and she ran in to see about him. He was not crying but only seemed frightened by the storm. But after that he changed from the sweet little boy into a very demanding and even cruel person at times. She immediately noticed the change because he always insisted on constantly wearing a hat after that peculiar night and no longer wanted to be called by his birth name Clarence Lee, but C.L. The unearthly sound he had made always haunted her and she was convinced that he was possessed by a strange energy ever since that night. Perhaps this was an explanation of his strange behavior.

C.L. was possessed! Now I understood. Not once did C.L. let me out of his sight. No longer did he allow me to go to the store alone. I do not remember how many times C.L. raped me. I did not care whether I lived or died; everything in life had lost its meaning.

When C.L. was not home, we would sit together at the table wishing something would happen to him, that he would never come home. Our plan was that as soon as C.L. was admitted to the hospital for his hernia operation, we would make our escape.

Image 1: The grandmother with whom Omnec spent her early years on Earth.

Image 2: The last school year, Omnec is 14 years old.

Chapter 2 – A Light at the End of the Tunnel

It was about eight o'clock one night when I came home. Immediately as I stepped into the living room, I knew they had been fighting again. Mom was sitting on a sofa, dazed. Her robe was torn. "What's the matter?" I asked her. She just looked at me without answering. Moments later I heard a knock and opened the front door. It was the man from the liquor store, with a fifth of vodka. I could not believe my eyes!

Whispering, because C.L. was in the bedroom, I said, "You know, really, this is the wrong time for you to bring this stuff. If you knew the situation here, you wouldn't bring it at all!"

"Why, what's the matter?" He stepped through the doorway.

"They just had a big fight", I explained. "See, you don't understand. They don't just drink socially. They drink every day." He came in and sat down near the door. "Well, if I would have known, I really wouldn't have come. I'm really sorry," he said sincerely. I sat down on the couch and whispered to the man that I had just gotten home myself and didn't know what was going on.

Just then C.L. came roaring out of the bedroom, staggering all over the place. "Yeah? You think I can't hear everything, huh. I'll teach you to whore around on me, both of you, cut your damn throats, that's what I'll do." Before any of us moved, C.L. was at the kitchen sink grabbing a long thin, ugly knife. He staggered toward my mother; in an instant I blocked his way. "C.L., please leave her alone," I pleaded.

He stared at me with burning hate in his eyes. "I'll cut your throat as quick as hers!" I shoved Donna into the bedroom, closing the door. C.L. stood there, amazed that I had the guts to defy him. "All right, you little bitch, I'll cut your throat too."

The liquor store man stood by flabbergasted, his mouth hanging open. Finally he decided to come over and help me. "No, please!" I cried. "Just turn off the lights. If you get involved it's worse than just a family quarrel."

I stood eye to eye with C.L. I knew that drunk as he was, he would not hesitate to kill me. "God, help me," I said as I lunged forward head first into his stomach. I grabbed for his wrists and shoved him backward, trying to wrestle the knife away. Blood started splashing all over the place. My panic gave me the strength to back C.L. against the wall and bang his wrist until the knife fell. With one last push, C.L. fell sideways against the door and into the bedroom. He crawled into bed mumbling.

I leaned against the wall, exhausted. Trembling and shaking I picked up the knife and looked into the bedroom. "Go ahead," C.L. drawled out, "cut my throat if you want to." "I'm not like you, C.L.," I said. "I've got more sense. I'm not trying to get even. I'm not violent 'cause I realize the consequences." C.L. was probably too drunk to understand me.

In the living room I poured a big glass of vodka. Maybe I wasn't going to kill him, but I sure enough would knock him out.

The liquor store man walked toward me. "Hey, I think you're hurt. There's blood all over you." "No, I think I'm all right," I said. "Maybe it was him that got hurt." Just then I heard C.L. again, choking Mom in the bedroom. "God, he just can't stop." He drank the vodka in one go and crashed back on the bed. Seconds later he had dozed off.

Weak and limp, I sat down again in the living room. "Look, you are hurt," the man said, pointing to a bloody slice in my side.

Coming home from the hospital that night with three stitches in my side, I entered my bedroom utterly defeated. Donna and C.L. were sound asleep. This was the bitter end – I could not take another day. I tried to be good, and I tried to be obedient, but every time I came home they would be at it again. By this time C.L. was taking to knives and broken beer bottles. When was it all going to end, I wondered? Tonight, perhaps?

I was so confused, so upset, and so hurt about the past months that I cried myself to sleep once again. Only this time my stomach was full of sleeping pills and a drink. I knew it was wrong, and as I got drowsy I begged forgiveness of God and of my people. I knew that suicide is not a solution but at that moment I couldn't see any other way out. Slowly I dozed off.

Waking the next morning was most perplexing; I was sure I would die. "Oh, thank goodness," I thought, "I must remember my mission and never be foolish again."

All of us had slept very late into the day. C.L. did not remember the previous night and I did not bother to tell him. Neither did I say anything to Mom because I wanted to save her from more suffering. Any day now she and I would be running away for good. No doubt about it, the man was deteriorating mentally, and we could not bear another day with him. Mom and I were so depressed by now that we hoped either he would die, or we would.

I felt as miserable and confused as ever. Knowing how peaceful and wonderful my life on Venus had been, made a rotten life here even worse. And yet I could understand that all of this was my choice. This was the kind of life Kanjuri and Vonic and Odin had been preparing me for. I know that my life on Venus helped me to survive without getting emotionally disturbed any more than I was. At least my attitude toward men had not become negative. I knew very well that most men were not like C.L.

During my dreams, sometimes when I was not so emotionally caught up in the events of the day, I visited with Arena and Odin. From them I received much encouragement. My life would get better, they said, and although it would perhaps take many years, I would find our spiritual teaching. Good will come from all the bad experiences, they assured me. In the future I will understand. Many many Earth people have suffered as I have, and because of this suffering, many people will be able to relate to me as a person instead of an alien.

In the afternoon, the hospital accepted C.L. for the hernia operation! The chance to escape C.L. was now upon us. We helped pack his things and escorted him there, and oh boy were we happy! But first we went to visit him, and feeling sorry that he was in so much pain, we took along a box of chocolates. C.L. was his usual self. He tried to choke my mother right there in the hospital.

That gave her the momentum to go ahead and write the list. It was a note to the doctor suggesting what he was to be checked for; C.L. approved it. Outside his room we added, “Check for mental disorders.”

So it seemed when the doctor called us that he would not be able to keep C.L. for the hernia operation because he did not have enough insurance to cover the surgery. “Should we transfer him to the County Hospital?” he asked. He knew very well that C.L. absolutely refused to ever be admitted to a county hospital. Instantly the light went on in Mom’s mind – she had the perfect solution. The doctor must convince C.L. that they were transferring him to a hospital with advanced techniques for his surgery, not letting him know that it was the county hospital which was for poor people with little or no money. Moments later the doctor was on the line again. All we needed to do was arrange with him and the ambulance drivers to keep the truth from C.L. He agreed. Later in the day Donna's nurse friend at the hospital called us. C.L. was safely in the ambulance, and our chance to get away was truly here.

For a short while, we lived with friends in a trailer park. Mom was so happy to be away from C.L. that she stopped drinking. I had never seen her so content as then. I was enjoying myself too. What a change to be able to forget my troubles and play with the kids. But I knew deep inside that C.L. would be after us. It would not be long before suspicious C.L. realized what had happened. Donna had made plans to leave Boulder City soon, but soon was not soon enough.

We were surely taken by surprise when Maria, one of Mom's fellow workers at the hospital, came running to our trailer one night. "Donna! C.L. is out!" she said between breaths. Horrified, we listened. "He went and completely tore apart the house you used to live in, jerked down the curtains, slit open the mattresses with knives, went completely crazy", she said. "The landlady called the police, but by the time they got there he was over at my house, said I knew where you were. He's got dynamite in the trunk – everything you could think of, shotguns, knives, and dynamite. He's looking for you and he's going to kill you and Sheila for putting him in the county hospital and running off. He said nobody can get away from him! You know, you don't have a chance. You've got to call the police, you've got to get out of here!"

Shaking with fear we called the Boulder City police and explained our situation. Maria witnessed to them that he did have dangerous materials and was apt to use them because he was crazy. After checking with the county hospital they immediately put out an alert on C.L. and came to pick us up. Three Boulder City squad cars arrived at the trailer park. Donna and I all got into the middle car. "Stay down on the floorboards. This man is dangerous", the officer instructed. "He's liable to throw dynamite or anything at the car if he sees you in it. So please stay down!"

Mom and I sat in the car with the officers, waiting in the parking lot behind the Boulder City Police Department. "We know he's dangerous, Mrs. Renald", one of the men said. "We checked his record 'cause we thought he really acted strange around this town, the way he never let your daughter out of his sight, and just in general the impression he made. We checked on him in all the states and the reports started coming through, till we had a whole list of things. But we can't hold him except for a crime he committed in Nevada."

By the time they came out to get us, the sun was starting to come up. "OK, you can get off now. We've got him in jail, Mrs. Renald. We finally caught him". What a relief. "How did you ever get him?" Mom asked. "Some service station attendant made a mistake, thought he was an escaped mental patient we were looking for", the officer explained. "He called us and we picked him up that way. We're holding him for carrying explosives", said the officer as we entered the station. The jails were downstairs.

Mom and I could hear him below. We just looked at each other, terror in our eyes. "Don't be afraid. He can't get out. He's raging right now and is really upset. But we have to have something to hold him on here, otherwise we'll have to let him go in twenty-four hours. We can't hold him any longer for possessing dangerous weapons. We've got a long list of things he supposedly did, hijacking, fraud, selling liquor without a license, even worse than that. But you have to have something on him in Nevada unless the authorities from other states come and get him. So you have to report any kind of crime he's done". I spoke up. "Well, we can report the fact that he tried to use a knife on my mother, and he did stab me". I showed them my scar. Mom was surprised! After we had done all the paperwork, they took our fingerprints and we were ready to leave. Just then the Chief of Police took me into a private office, alone. "Excuse us a moment, please", he said to Mom.

"Um, would you tell me, Sheila, if C.L. ever raped you?" he asked. "No, he hasn't!" I blurted out automatically. "Look, Sheila, you don't have to be afraid to tell me the truth, because he's not going to hurt you. Statutory rape is a big crime in Nevada. But we can't hold him long even on the family thing with the knife. We can only hold him on assault and battery, but if he gets out it's really going to be tough on us and you too. You have to tell me the truth while there is time".

I kept silent. My thoughts run wild. What should I do? "Look, Sheila, I'm not a dumbbell. Boulder City is a very small town. I've noticed that he never let you have any friends, never even let you out of his sight. I've never seen you by yourself. And the way you go to the store and rush back to your house, something is really fishy. No grown man acts that way normally about his daughter. So we know something is wrong, but we can't do anything until we have a written statement from you".

"Yes, it's true", I broke out crying. Terribly embarrassed and upset, I told the Chief about that first day, and that I didn't know how many times he had done it since then, because I didn't want to know!

"But why didn't you tell your mother?" he asked. After I explained the whole story about Pap and Mom and C.L., the Chief stepped out of the room for a few minutes. Then he called me out. Mom was crying. "Sheila, how come you never told me. Why didn't you tell me what C.L. did to you?"

"Mommy, I was afraid to", I said, choking over my words. "I wasn't sure you'd believe me. I was afraid C.L. would tell you I did it and then you would hate me, and I didn't want you to hate me. He said you'd believe I led him on". Both of us cried and clung to each other. "Sheila", she sobbed, "I'll never hate you, Sheila. If there's anybody I hate, it's him. If I would have known what he did, I would have taken a pistol and blown his brains out. I can't blame you 'cause it's true – I've been accusing you of it in my jealous mind. But I wish you would have told me. It would have made things easier. I do love you more than my life, Sheila".

We looked at each other. Mom was terribly upset and haggard, blamed herself for everything. At last she knew why I suddenly had started drinking alcohol.

The police took me immediately to the hospital where the doctor checked my story. How humiliating it was to go in at this age, among all the people I was once worked with. I was definitely not a virgin any longer, the doctor told my mother, and it was not long ago that it had happened.

At the police station the Chief took us into his office. "I hate to tell you Sheila, I hate to embarrass you, but you have to write word for word in your own handwriting what he did, for the report. Otherwise it's not valid."

Painfully I wrote word for word what C.L. had done that morning, how he held me down after beating me and tearing my pajama, how he kept asking, "Don't you like it?" while I just lay there with tears streaming from my eyes.

"Well, this is enough to hold him", the Chief said. "We'll have to get you a lawyer and everything, but that will be in Las Vegas 'cause this is a state thing". The officer paused. "Sheila, even though it was painful for you, we have to hold this man because he is a danger to society, not just to you and your mother, but to everybody else. He's probably done this many times and gotten away with it".

The Boulder City Chief of Police came along with me the day I was to see the lawyer in Las Vegas, one of the state's attorneys. He went in to speak with the man while I took my first lie detector's test. It took a long time for me to relax in order for the device to deliver relevant results. Until I was relaxed enough, everything was a lie. Then the drill began.

"Are you sure you haven't made love to any other boy? Are you sure of this, are you sure of that?" It was horrible.

In legal terms my case was one of statutory rape, State of Nevada versus C.L. Renald. This was the reason for seeing a state's attorney. He seemed to be a very nice man, as sympathetic as he could be. "Now Sheila", he began, "we have had a lot of these cases before. You have to be really sincere. You don't want to lie about a person. I'm not saying that you are, because I really believe you. But we have a lot of scrupulous people, the people who will be the jury, the judge – all these people don't know you. They don't know your situation. A lot of men have been trapped this way, so they're not necessarily going to be sympathetic. They're going to have to be detached from the whole thing. You're going to have to try to win them over".

One of the attorneys from the office of the state's attorney should handle my case. It would be some time, said my lawyer, before the whole mess would be cleared up. Until then I would have to be in school, because it was against the law for a girl of my age not to be enrolled. My stomach turned. Their reasoning was very simple. The state could not provide a lawyer if I myself was breaking the law. Nevertheless, I cringed at the thought having to go back at school.

I knew I was in school only for a short time and I surely could not bring myself to studying seriously. My teachers were amazed nevertheless to see how quickly I caught up with the rest of the class. In mathematics I was at the head of the class. But I felt out of place.

Some weeks later our first hearing took place in Boulder City. I testified that C.L. had attacked both my mother and myself, threatening to kill me with a knife. I showed them my scar and the hospital papers. The liquor store man verified my story.

C.L. flew into a rage, calling me a damn liar, while at the same time his counsel tried to quiet him down. The judge reprimanded C.L. for talking out of turn, said he could get into trouble for that, too. C.L. looked terribly pale and sick. Being an outdoor type of person, locking him up could almost kill him, especially since he already had such a bad liver from drinking all his life.

"Don't feel sorry for him", one of the police officers said. "That's the worst thing you could do because then you get yourself into trouble. He's a human being, but he is also a criminal, and the fact is that he is dangerous to more people than you. So, for heaven's sake, don't talk about feeling sorry for him".

Walking to school one morning with a bunch of kids, a car drove up alongside and stopped. Two shotguns pointed out the window toward my head. The thugs said to me that C.L. may be in jail and could not do anything, but his friends weren't in jail. And they would kill me if I testified in court. I was utterly horrified. I took off running, afraid these guys would shoot me in the back. The other kids just stood there with their mouths open as the car squealed away.

"What was that all about", they asked. "It was just a joke!" I said shakily, trying to force a smile.

I called my lawyer that day and told him what happened, that I was afraid I was being watched. I refused to go to school another day. "You'll have to keep going to school, Sheila, but we'll have detectives escort you", he assured me. That's how I went to and from school every day, until school let out in June.

What else could I think when Mom didn't come home one night, except that these guys had caught up with her? She finally returned in the morning, just in ecstasy, smiling and cheery. I was crying and carrying on, telling how much I had worried she was dead.

"Oh, honey, I'm sorry... I really didn't mean to worry you", she said, hugging me. "You know, Mommy wouldn't have worried you for anything in the world, but I met someone

I really like. We're going to get married, and we're going to Chicago".

"But I can't go to Chicago. I have to go to court".

"Well, that's all right. I can leave you here if you want to stay, with the Fishmans", Mom offered. And that was that.

During all these times I often used the memory of my wonderful Aunt Arena, Uncle Odin, and all my lovely friends as a cushion to fall back on. Whenever I could close my eyes and see my beautiful home and feel their love and caring, I knew all my suffering would be worthwhile if I could share these memories with Earth's people. Each night I thanked the Supreme Deity for the strength to go on.

Chapter 3 – Chicago

Shortly afterwards I met the new guy in Mom's life: Pedro. He lived at a nearby trailer park. It was only a short walking distance away. On our way there, she told me all about him. Pedro and Donna had met in a bar and fell in love on first sight. Pedro was crazy about her, wanted to take her out to dinner, but they ended up going shopping for mushrooms and steaks and wine. Then he took Mom to his trailer and fixed a fabulous steak dinner. This was when she stayed away all night.

Pedro turned out to be a really sweet little man, and very handsome. A slim frame and dark features showed his Spanish heritage. He had brown eyes and the typical long, graceful Spanish nose and a dark thick mustache, also black curly hair. Compared to C.L.'s lumbering hulk he was a small man. The important thing was that he loved Mom and seemed to be kind and considerate. I could tell he had a lot of pride and inherited ideas.

He was from a rich family in Chihuahua, Mexico. His first wife bore him five children and I suppose he ran around on her, for she threw him out one day. He went to the States, working as a busboy and dishwasher, and then waiter. He saved his money for Barber college. Now that he had become a Master Barber and stylist of razor cutting, he worked at the Las Vegas airport. But his dream was to go to Chicago to open his own shop. Mom was excited and for her I was happy. They had married in Las Vegas less than a month after they had met. They stayed in his trailer until they left for Illinois. And I stayed with the Fishmans.

In the meantime, there had been another court date, where the rape charges against C.L. were made. C.L. stood in front of the judge and denied everything. I noticed he had lost a lot of weight. They told me he had refused to eat until a doctor put him on a special diet; and drying up from alcohol was not easy.

When school started in September, I was driven every day by the Fishman's teenage son Henry. He and I were enrolled in the same high school. For a while our romance blossomed, but more or less it was he who had a crush on me, although I did like him very much as a friend. We spent a great deal of time together. More and more I enjoyed having relationships with people my own age.

The girls in our high school sewing class were treated to a tea party by McCall's, the well-known fashion magazine. Although they were interested in our dress patterns, they seemed to be more intrigued with me than with the patterns I had created. McCall's offered me, to my utter surprise, a career in modeling and a three-year contract, both of which I accepted after gaining permission from the State's attorney's office. My lawyer agreed that I would not need to finish school because McCall's offered such basic courses as math, history and English to me and other young models.

One of the ways McCall's checked to see whether I was mentally and physically healthy for modeling was to send me to a psychiatrist. When he asked me about myself, I decided to try out the truth on him. After listening very patiently and silently, the man came to a conclusion which he did not hesitate to tell me. This story of my life on Venus was a product of my imagination, resulting from a very unhappy childhood that I could not adjust to. I had created my own world in which to seek comfort.

I replied that I was not offended by his conclusion, because the key to all material things, to all the wonders of man's world, is the imagination. I went on to explain that everything manmade first exists in someone's imagination before it is created in the physical world.

The psychiatrist just looked at me, didn't know what to think, didn't know what to say. He could not argue with that and seemed very upset. McCall's received a very good report from him, without mention of Venus because this was a confidential matter. The psychiatrist stated that I was a well-balanced young lady able to accept and handle problems, and that I did not have any deep emotional problems.

The remainder of my stay in Nevada was a time of seeing many new places, for with the photographers and equipment crew we traveled to scenic parts of California, Arizona, and Nevada. Instead of going to school every day, I worked one or two days each week and was paid very well. My career with McCall's ended shortly after I and three other girls appeared on the cover. The State attorney's office requested that the contract be voided because my being out of town so often conflicted with appearing in court.

One day a policeman walked up, stern-faced as he could be. "Are you Sheila Gibson, Hodgson, Renald, MacLellan?"

"Yes", I said.

"Boy, you sure do have a lot of aliases for a young girl your age!" He laughed. That was impressive, he told me. Then he presented the subpoena. I understood from all the legal-sounding jargon that it was very important for me to show up at C.L.'s trial. My lawyer gave me the same advice; hold on to that subpoena and don't let anything happen to it. Our court dates would be starting pretty soon.

Just then I received a letter from Donna, saying that she was terribly ill and needed my help. Would I come to Chicago for a few weeks before my court date? I asked my lawyer if this was O.K. with him. Yes, he said, but I was to stop by and see him before I left.

My lawyer presented his card to me. "We'll pay your fare back, so if anything happens that you can't come back, be sure to call me. You can fly back ... you have to get here in time because C.L. has been in jail for a long time now and all the court dates are set up. Then we can put him away for awhile".

I thanked him and said goodbye. Once more I entered a bus to go across the country to a new state.

Looking out the bus window, the first I saw of Chicago was the cold, the gray, the ugly. "How horrible this place is!" I thought, "compared to the sunny desert and open space." I have changed my mind since then. Today I think Chicago is one of the country's most beautiful cities.

Stepping from the bus at the huge, monstrous-looking bus station, I was completely lost. "Where in the hell are they?" I wondered. "Where am I supposed to be going? Who am I supposed to call?" And I was worried about Mom, too. I went upstairs and saw a waiting area, so I decided that the best move was to sit down and wait. Droves of people buzzed all over the place. "Sheila!" I heard my name being called.

Mom and Pedro were almost upon me before I saw them. "Hi, Mommy, how are you?"

"Much better, Hon`", she replied. My mother looked unusually healthy. "We thought this girl in a cowboy suit was you and we took after her."

I didn't know whether to be happy or sad. I felt she had never been sick, and her letter was only a trick to lure me away from Nevada.

Right after we got home Mom wanted to see my subpoena. Hesitantly I handed it to her. I froze, just stared as she tore it up right before my eyes.

"What are you doing?!" I cried in horror and surprise.

"I'm not going to let you appear against C.L."

"But why?"

"Because I'm afraid he'll kill you!" Donna said intensely. I stood there dumbfounded. "I'm not afraid to appear in court against him".

It was no use to argue. “You’re not afraid but I am”, my mother said. “I’m afraid for you because I know C.L. After living with him for ten years I know him better than you”.

Pedro agreed with her that I should not go back to Nevada, and for the moment I let the matter drop. In my mind I was determined to call my lawyer as soon as I was alone, but it turned out that I could not find his card in my purse the next day. Mom and Pedro must have sneaked it out.

I resigned myself to writing the Fishmans for the rest of my clothes, and realized that I would probably never see them again. My life in Chicago was beginning on a sour note.

Our one-room furnished apartment did not look much better than the building it was in, rickety and broken-down. It was really nothing but a sleeping room. I learned that Mom and Pedro always went out to the little Mexican restaurant next door. Mom made an effort to explain that life would be uncomfortable for a while; but soon we would be moving to a better place. She and Pedro were still saving their money for a barbershop, while Pedro went to barber school to be licensed here in Illinois. In the meantime, he worked as a stylist or Master Barber.

I did not care much for Pedro; something about him bothered me, but I did not know what it was. I had to admit, though, that he was always friendly and generous and that living with him was obviously good for my mother.

What bothered me most of all about our new apartment was that we all had to sleep together in the same bed; I slept against the wall, as close to it as I could. Along the wall ran an exposed water pipe with a faucet, which I accidentally turned on one night while turning over. Water was gushing across the bed, soaking all of us before anyone could figure out what was happening. I must say that there is nothing quite like a shower in bed, in the middle of a winter night...

There were times when I would wake up in the dark of night with the haunting feeling that someone was touching me. But when I woke up fully, Donna and Pedro were sleeping peacefully. "Maybe it's just my imagination", I thought. "Maybe I'm just dreaming." I did not pay much attention to it because I trusted Pedro at the time, and I just assumed that my sleeping with all these people affected my dreams.

We had not lived at the apartment for much more than a week after I arrived, when Pedro took us to see the new barbershop. It was located in the middle of a busy Jewish district. The shop was such a mess that we spent several days cleaning and mopping and painting. Pedro ordered new barber chairs and replaced the tile floor.

I learned to my dismay that in order to save money we would be living in the back room, which was once a beauty shop. After spending a day or two fixing it up, our new home was ready. Mom and Pedro had their own bed, thank heaven, and I was to sleep on the couch out in the hall leading to the shop. A two-burner hot plate served as our kitchen. For bathing we used a foot tub which was filled by connecting a hose to the faucet of a small sink. The bathroom was near the back entrance.

Before long, business was going very well. Pedro was an excellent barber and became well known for his good work. People liked him. Being a very generous person, Pedro let us go shopping, took us out to dinner and the movies. Almost anything seemed better than our life with C.L. Every once in a while Pedro and Mom drank, but there wasn't any fighting. So I really didn't have much reason to be worried.

At first, Pedro did not allow me to have any boyfriends, but Mom raised such a fuss over this that he gave in. My social life continued full speed ahead, and I soon had lots of boyfriends. I was very young and not serious about anything or anyone at the time. I wanted to be free more than anything else.

I found myself a waitressing job. I enjoyed this work and I did not consider it a lowly position. At the same time, I started to do freelance-modeling in Chicago. My first job was for White Rain Shampoo, while they made cardboard posters of me to set up in the stores. The best-paying job was a sweatshirt ad for Playboy; it brought me about $ 300 each month for a year. A Levi's commercial for television also paid well. Sometimes I worked two to three times a week, and then there were times when I worked only a couple of times per month.

I had often wondered what happened to C.L. and wished that I could have testified in court. We did know that C.L. had been released. A letter from him arrived from Tennessee; he had given it to Grandma who in turn sent it to us. His words told us how sick he was: "Sheila, baby, I don`t know how you could say all those things about me..." It seemed that he had trouble accepting what he had done. I never saw him or heard of him again after that letter.

After a while, Mom and Pedro started drinking and fighting more. The fighting was not so bad, but I saw that Pedro was getting into the habit of beating my mother. He got meaner and meaner, accusing me of being a queer when I went out with girlfriends, and making nasty remarks when I dated men.

Pedro began to take full advantage of the times that Mom was drunk or half-drunk. I had to fight him all over the place, kicking and screaming, while he persisted in trying to rape me. Just about every time, I ended up locking myself in the bathroom until Pedro had gone to sleep.

Pedro took me out to dinner once when Mom was sick in bed with ulcers. On our way home he tried every possible scheme to convince me to go into a hotel with him, short of bodily dragging me there. Disgusted and feeling a strange sick sensation in the pit of my stomach, I later told Mom about what had happened.

I realized that the time had come for me to move out on my own. "I want to move out before any trouble starts", I said to Mom, "because I don't want to go through the same thing as with C.L."

Mom disagreed. "But you're too young. You can't move out on your own" "Well, I'll be sixteen pretty soon and I do have a job. Besides, I love you and I want things to be different. I think we are all too close here and have too little privacy".

"You'll get into trouble", Pedro warned, "But I'm not going to stop you".

Less than a week later I had found a one-bedroom apartment on Sheridan Road. It wasn't the nicest place in town, but at least I was away from Pedro. On the day I moved out, I went to the bank to withdraw my savings. After signing for the apartment, I had $ 100 left, and I rode to work on the bus. I walked through the doors of the restaurant, said hello to my coworkers, and stopped dead in my tracks. My purse! All my money, my apartment keys, everything was on the bus! On picking up my shopping bags I had left my purse on the seat.

"Oh, horrors!" I raced out the doors and rushed up to the first car I saw. Not seeing me, the man drove off. Then I saw a police waiting for a red light across the street. I dashed through the traffic and hastily explained my predicament to the startled officer.

"Jump in the back", he ordered without hesitation. The officer made a U-turn and flipped on his siren and flashing lights. We raced down Lawrence Avenue; the bus looked hopelessly tiny in the distance. Speeding along, we came close to running down two nuns who were crossing the street.

Just then I realized with apprehension that we were approaching the barbershop. And it was just my luck that we had a red light at the intersection. The police officer slowed down, sirens warning the traffic to let us pass.

Looking up, Pedro saw me sitting in back of the squad car. His razor dropped and he dashed for the phone. "Oh, no!" I thought fearfully. But right now my attention was riveted on the bus, and I worried that I would never see my purse again.

When the bus stopped for a red light, we pulled in front and screeched to a stop at an angle, sirens still running. Seeing both of us jump out, the bus driver was terrified, thinking he was under arrest but not knowing what for. He knew that the police rarely ran down busses.

The frightened driver threw up his hands. I ran to the back of the bus ... and it was still there! My purse was still there! Perhaps no one had seen the little clutch bag because it was the same color as the seat.

Meanwhile, the policeman tried to calm the bus driver: "Put your hands down. You're not under arrest", he said laughingly. The driver said, "I tell you, you scared me to death!"

On our way back, the policeman lectured me. "Let this be a lesson to you, young lady, because not every policeman will do this for you. You've got to be more careful with your things; you're lucky your purse was still there. But it was exciting for me too. I had a lot of fun".

Everyone in the restaurant was stunned. They had seen me walking in, racing out, approaching a man's car just driving off, and dashing into a police car to follow in the same direction. They were wondering if the man had done something to warrant being chased. Totally puzzled they awaited my return.

Back at work, everybody crowded around me: "What happened? What did the man do?" "What man?" I asked, completely perplexed.

"That man who drove off, and you took off after him in a police car".

"He didn't do anything!" I was surprised to hear how they had been waiting in suspense. "I was going to ask him to try and help me catch the bus because I left my purse on it, and when he drove off I saw the police car".

Everyone thought it was a hilarious scene.

Finally I called my mother. She was furious. "Pedro almost cut a man's ear off when he saw you! We were both nervous wrecks". As I told her the story, Mom began to laugh. But Pedro remained furious. "See, I told you she'd get into trouble if she moved out on her own. And it's only the first day".

The freedom of living on my own was well worth the money it cost me to take care of myself. I came and went where I pleased and when I pleased. And I enjoyed all the friends I cared to have. This was a new way of life for me, and I relished it. Just being away from Pedro's drunken passes was heavenly.

Modeling jobs brought me a great deal more money than I really needed, and I spent most of it foolishly. I would throw the clothes away and buy new ones instead of washing them. And I would take all my friends out to eat steaks, and I ate out myself all the time.

This was a time of my life where I became more and more interested in parties and socializing, because C.L. never allowed me to have friends and we never lived in one place long enough to know anyone.

I soon had a bad reputation on my floor of the building, thanks to the wild parties and goings on, and to my unawareness of how reputations get started – people are inclined to believe that if you have noisy parties then there is sure to be alcohol and sex.

As time went on, my parties became wilder and wilder. The wildest party of all took place shortly before Mom and Pedro forced me to move back to the barbershop. The reason so many people showed up was that I had told all the students who came into the restaurant that they were cordially invited.

A sign decorated my apartment door on that memorable night. "Boys – take off your shirts before you come in". The whole idea was that we would throw all the shirts in the middle of the floor, and each girl would pick one up; its owner was to be her dancing partner.

The craziest game of all gave each girl a turn in the dark closet. All of the boys stood in a circle in the living room, while one of us spun around in the center, pointing. Then the girl in the closet would yell, "Stop!" At that moment, whichever boy was pointed at would have a turn in the closet with her, for five minutes by the clock. It was harmless fun for not too much can happen in five minutes!

Drinking the fermented apple cider I had made, made all of us noisier by the minute. Some of the guys had of course brought their booze which they had stashed outside on the fire escape, unknown to me at the time. When the police finally arrived (called no doubt by our neighbors who found that stuffing cotton in their ears didn't help) my apartment was a wreck. The officer assumed the worst. But he was fair and gave me a chance to explain.

"Well, it's a harmless party", he admitted after I had done the talking. He took me out into the hall. "Sheila, you know how these old people are, they don't like this sort of stuff because it disturbs them. Just keep it quiet and we'll let it go at that".

I thanked him and returned to give the news to the ones who were capable of hearing, and I tried to shush them. Our party came to a final rest at 7:30 in the morning.

At nine I was woken by the shrill ringing of the phone and looked around. Here were people, left and right, sleeping. Four or five other boys and girls were stretched across my bed with me. One guy was lying under the couch, and another guy was sleeping in the bathtub. The closets were being used, too. I had people wall to wall. I dragged myself to the telephone. It was Mom. How was I, she asked. I could barely talk, or hold open my eyes, but I managed to say all was okay. She didn't become suspicious. But the elderly lady, who lived next door and who had called the police, some days later took advantage of her chance to send me home. I was down the hall, visiting with friends when my phone rang and the same old lady entered my apartment to answer it. Mom was on the line. "If you care anything about your daughter", the old lady lectured, "you'll come and get her. She's a little prostitute. She's got guys in and out all the time."

They were waiting for me after I returned from work that day. I was ordered back to the barbershop, on grounds that I was underage and that Mom had custody of me. I didn't like this at all, and I was very unhappy, but seeing that Pedro would not let up until I came home, I moved back to the barbershop even thought I didn't feel safe there. "We can't have you getting into any more trouble", they said, sounding concerned.

When Mom told me about the phone call, I asked, "Why would that lady say that; just because I have lots of friends doesn't mean I have sex with them all?"

Mom explained to me what a prostitute was, and how if you had too many boys in and out of your apartment that it did not look right, no matter if you were innocent or not. I learned that in Earth's society it was frowned upon to invite men to your place if you lived alone.

Again I had learned an important lesson about life on Earth.

My reputation was bad because I had let boys stay in my apartment if they got into trouble at home, and their girlfriends, too. Not many young people were so independent. At their age they were in school and lived with parents. Anyone as young as I with living in an apartment on her own was popular. “Oh!” I exclaimed. “If this is how people think, no wonder they thought I was bad”. Just a few days after I had moved back to the barbershop, we traveled together to El Paso, Texas, where Pedro dropped us off at a hotel and went on to visit his family in Mexico.

It was the second-last day of our stay in El Paso, when I left the hotel in the evening to order some food and drinks from our favorite restaurant, while Mom waited for my return with a ravenous appetite.

As I sat in the booth waiting for my order, I noticed that a handsome young man in an army uniform with black hair and blue eyes kept staring at me. I glanced around to see whether he was staring at someone else, but he was not.

Presently he came over and said hello. He was not trying to make a pass at me, he explained, but he was an artist who thought I was the most beautiful girl he had ever seen. My facial features, my eyes, my nose, everything was balanced. My long neck and beautiful hair was just perfect. “May I do your portrait some day?” he asked meekly. I was speechless and very flattered. He walked me back to our hotel and told me a little bit about himself. Carl was his name and he was of German descent. Being able to speak German fluently he was presently stationed in Germany. As I thought he was very likeable, I told him that I would be glad to come down and meet him in the park the next day at noon, and let him do my portrait.

I told my mother about Carl, and we both were all excited about seeing him the next day. But Pedro came home that night to pop my balloon; we would be leaving at ten o'clock in the morning. The next morning, we learned that our train did not leave until two o'clock. I felt like an emotional yo-yo. Close to noon I sneaked out of the hotel with my name and address on a slip of paper. I ran barefoot over to the park. Carl was waiting for me already.

"Carl, I'm sorry but I can't pose for you because my stepfather came back and he is not the type of person who would understand. He told me not to talk to anybody here". I caught my breath. "But I like you very much and I'd like you to write me if you'd like to".

Carl just stood there looking sadly at me. "How sad we don't have more time together", he said. "I just learned that I have to go back to Germany today. And I just came here to let you know and not keep you waiting in vain. I'll write you because I like you very much, too. I've seen women all over the world but I've never seen one as beautiful as you", he said softly. "I don't know how to thank you". I was embarrassed. I ran back to the hotel, and that was the last I saw of him.

Every month thereafter I received a letter from Carl, from Germany where he was stationed. With every letter, Carl sent along a sketch of German scenes, of castles he had visited. And he included photos of himself. I in turn sent Carl modeling photographs of myself, such as the one where they had posed me like Marilyn Monroe in a black, low-cut tight dress and push-up bra. Lacey garters showed as I partly pulled up my dress. Carl liked that one best of all; it made all the guys he knew crazy about me, he said.

In our letters we discussed our spiritual beliefs, family life, children, education, marriage, and we found that we agreed on many things, and that we had many likes and dislikes in common. He was very excited about this and finally asked if I would marry him. I consented. I loved Carl, too, even though we had spent so little time together. I felt we had known and loved each other in past life-times.

In the next letter, Carl announced that he had bought an uncut two-carat diamond, and asked how I wanted to have it set. He was planning to send me an engagement ring. A one and one-tenth carat solitaire set in platinum with a white gold band arrived in a mailbox. All my friends gasped over its beauty, and I of course was overjoyed.

Our plan was that during the following summer I would come to Germany and we would be married there. When I heard all of this I began to feel guilty about my past, about the fact that I was no longer a virgin. I wrote Carl that I could not marry him until he knew the truth. My stepfather had raped me at fourteen and I was no longer a virgin. A telegram arrived from Germany. "The past does not matter. I love you now, as you are now. Love, Carl"

Although I knew him only through letters, and he never touched or kissed me, it made no difference. I loved Carl and eagerly looked forward to the coming summer. With the money he sent me, I went shopping for all the things I needed, especially the wedding gown. After not finding the gown of my dreams, I designed my own and then had a dressmaker bring it into physical being. It was a dream in silk and lace. The lacey veil had a crown of pearls.

I wrote Carl that my mother and stepfather were drinking and fighting more than they ever did. Pedro continued to try bothering me and I was worried about staying there. I had the uncomfortable feeling that something terrible was about to happen.

Carl answered immediately. If Pedro ever hurt me, he would kill him, he said. I had kept Carl up-to-date on the family problem by letter.

It happened one night, when Mom staggered drunkenly to her bed and passed out. Pedro began picking on me. "So you think you're going to get married and leave me with her drunk like this all the time? You're not going to go off and leave me responsible for her", he yelled.

"She wouldn't be drunk if you hadn't bought her the stuff, Pedro!" I remarked. "And you know, you can't possess both Donna and me. You are married to my mother and you have to realize that". One cannot reason with a drunken man, I learned. Pedro was cursing he was going to kill me anyway, so he went off to the front of the shop, shouting he would shoot us both. As I went through the door leading to the shop, I realized that I could trap him in the barbershop by knocking it down. It was a heavy sliding door; too heavy for him to lift it back onto the rollers in his drunken state. But first I had to grab his keys, so that he could not remove the gun from the locked drawer, or leave the barbershop and enter from the rear. Then I planned to run back and slam the door behind me, hard enough that it would fall.

Fortunately, the barbershop was dark except for our neon business sign in front. Pedro never turned on the lights at night because we were not supposed to be living on the business premises.

I saw Pedro at the front of the shop fumbling with the keys of the drawer. Running up behind him, I grabbed them, and made a mad dash back to safety. Over the foot extension of the last barber chair I tripped, slamming into the door and knocking it from the hinges. The dark of night was not my friend after all. I was stuck!

Pedro bounded toward me and snatched the keys up from the floor, as I struggled to my feet with my hurt head reeling from the spill. He returned with the gun, waving it, prepared to kill me.

Lunging up I shoved him backwards and dashed toward the front of the shop, thinking I would break the plate glass window and get out to call for help on the street. I never made it that far. I was halfway up to the front door when he shot.

I felt a horrible pain, as if somebody had poured liquid metal onto my arm. I was terrified into freezing dead in my tracks, awaiting the next bullet to finish me off.

I turned around and went to sit down, shaking from head to foot. This man was drunk, had no control over himself. Sure of himself, Pedro came up and held the gun against my temple, pulling the trigger back. "Are you going to do what

I say? Or do you want to die?" he said with clenched teeth, unconcerned that he had hurt me.

I really did not feel it was time to die. I remembered how I had been unable to commit suicide because of my future mission on Earth. For the moment I forgot about being brave, knowing that with the first shot, drunk as he was, Pedro could have killed me and perhaps intended to, but missed. I decided that it was better to be raped than to be killed.

He took me to the back, within the shadows, and forced me to lie down on the floor. It seemed that the torture went on and on without end as I lay there crying. I did not think he would ever stop. I tried to close my eyes and think of someone I loved, but it was no use.

Feeling humiliated and used, I asked myself, "Why must I go through this? Have I been so ruthless and horrible to people (in my past lives) to deserve this treatment?"

When Pedro finished, he got up saying nothing. He straightened his clothes and ordered me up, with the gun in his hand. I was in a daze; my arm was hurting badly. I walked slowly to the sink across the shop and washed the blood from my arm and my hands. The bullet had barely entered the arm and fell into the sink. I found some gauze and tape in the medicine cabinet in the bathroom and bandaged the wound. I cried myself to sleep and slept most of the next day, a Sunday. Mom asked about my arm. I made up a lame story about tripping over one of the foot rests on the barber chairs while carrying empty beer bottles and cutting myself as I fell and broke one. She was concerned and helped me re-bandage it.

Pedro pretended nothing had happened. He had probably been too drunk to remember anything. I thought about Carl. "I'll never tell him, or anyone. He knows I am not a virgin anymore". I did not want to hurt my mother – that was one of my biggest problems. Too often I worried about and tried to protect my mother, instead of caring for myself. I loved her so much that I forgot myself over it.

Image 3: Omnec's Earth mother Donna with David.

Image 4: Donna, Omnec's Earth mother.

Image 5: Omnec at the age of 17, a few months after JoJo's birth.

Chapter 4 – Longing for Love and Understanding

Some weeks later, I began to get violently sick in the mornings. Until two o'clock every day none of the food I ate stayed in my stomach. But then I was fine for the rest of the day. I was worried and went to see a doctor after a few days.

"Well, you are pregnant, Sheila", he said with certainty. Almost three months after Pedro raped me I found out I was pregnant. I broke down crying.

"What's the matter?" the doctor asked.

"I'm engaged to be married and I just don't know what to do".

"Well, isn't it the boy's child?" he asked, puzzled.

"No, I haven't been sleeping with anybody. My stepfather raped me", I sobbed.

After I had told him the whole story, he quieted me down and offered to help me.

The doctor asked if I wanted to have an abortion, but I reasoned with him that if I could get pregnant just like that in one night, then this child has to be born for a reason. If I had been sleeping with someone over a period of time and then gotten pregnant, I might have felt different. No, I did not want an abortion.

I was afraid to tell Mom and Pedro, who were waiting outside. Finally, the moment came. The doctor brought Pedro and Mom into his office and we broke the news to them. Pedro tried to deny it at first. "Are you sure it's mine?"

"Pedro, how could you even ask such a thing? I don't blame you if you don't remember it, but I don't have any reason to lie", I said, sobbing. "I can't blame it on anyone else because you know I haven't been going out with anyone. I'm engaged to be married. If it was another boy I'd certainly admit it, because I wouldn't want to hurt Mommy."

Pedro finally admitted that he hazily remembered some of the details of that night, but when I did not say anything the next day, he assumed innocence of any wrongdoing. Pedro then offered to pay all the hospital bills if I in turn gave him the child.

On the way home everybody felt bad. Mom kept saying it was all her fault. Crying, she told me how she and Pedro had planned to get me pregnant so that they could have a baby, because she was not able to become pregnant again. It just shocked me so badly to hear this. It sounded incredible; how could anyone do such a thing, I thought in horror. "Sheila, I'm sorry", she sobbed, "but at the time I was drinking too much." In her blurred mind it was also a way of keeping me with her, for she still felt bad about having sent me away to Grandma and not seeing me for so many of my growing years.

What would I tell Carl now, so close to our planned marriage? How was he going to react to the fact of my getting raped a second time? Would he believe it? Who would believe it? With these questions flowing through my mind, I felt helpless, disgusted, and hurt.

Many people say that a woman cannot be raped in the first place. But the fact is that I know differently. Before that night I could close my legs and kick, and he had never gotten anywhere. But with a gun it is different.

"How am I going to get out of this mess?" I asked my mother, thinking of Carl.

Mother was quiet for a moment, then suggested, "Why don't you write and tell him I'm pregnant, and you have to stay to take care of me?"

I wrote Carl, saying that my mother had always wanted children, and that now after an operation she was pregnant. But it was a delicate situation, the doctor had said, and suggested that I stay with her until the child was born. It might be emotionally disturbing if I left for Germany. I would not be able to leave for another five months. Carl was not too happy about this, but it was all right if I stayed. He would wait for me.

My friends in the meantime tried to persuade me to send Pedro to jail, but Mom begged me not to. She loved him. I agreed not to call the police, but only on one promise, that they would not drink or fight anymore, because I could not stand it. “I cannot be so nervous carrying a baby. Any more fighting or arguments, I’m gone. I will not stay here!” I burst out in sobs from fright and nerves. Things improved for a while.

After four months of being pregnant, nothing showed. I was just as flat-tummied as ever. Of course I did not eat well; I was craving polish sausage and potato chips. I did not know much about nutrition, and I was not aware of the poisonous preservatives in food at that time.

Pedro kept up his game of bothering me while Mom was deep asleep or drinking. I would fight, and tell him to leave me alone; I begged, I cried, but he never stopped trying. One day, Mom asked if Pedro was bothering me. She suspected this. “No, he hasn’t”, I said, trying to protect her from the truth. Mom did not believe me. “Don’t lie to me, Sheila. I’m not going to say anything”. That was what I worried about, Pedro and Mom getting into a raging battle about it. “Yes he is; he won’t leave me alone”, I admitted. “But I can stand it until the baby is born, for your sake.”

But when I got home that day from work, they were drunk and had been fighting. Beer cans were strewn all over the place. No doubt Donna had broken her promise and jumped on Pedro. It made me angry because she had promised that this was the one thing she would not do. I pretended everything was all right, but I knew that somehow I had to leave.

"I'm going to the Laundromat to do the clothes", I said, getting busy.

Pedro looked up. "That's all right, you can do it tomorrow".

"No, I want to do them now because tomorrow is my day off". My plan was to throw all the laundry into the washers and take off. I had to go away; I could not tolerate this any longer. Kissing Mom goodbye and taking some money, I went out the door.

At the Laundromat, I put all the clothes into the washers, wondering what a person did in a situation like this. After transferring them to the dryers, I went for a walk, until I came to the bridge over the river. There I stood, crying, tears streaming down my face. "Where am I going? What in the world am I going to do? How am I going to get out of this? Uncle Odin, help me, please!"

A car pulled up just then, and a nicely-dressed man walked over. "You're not planning to jump, are you?" he asked worriedly.

"Oh, no, nothing like that", I sobbed. He persisted. "Well, something is wrong. I can see it. What's the matter, won't you talk to me?"

"No, it's all right, it's nothing", I said, starting to walk away.

The man walked along. "You can talk to me and confide in me, after all, I am a policeman. I'm off duty right now." Silence.

"Can I give you a lift somewhere?" "Well, I'm just at the Laundromat", I replied.

I got into the car with him and I told him everything, about Pedro raping me, that I was pregnant, that I wanted to leave, but that I was afraid to leave because he might kill my mother and I would be responsible. He listened until I was through. "Sheila, you have to leave", he concluded. "You can't stay there. I think the problem you've had all your life is that you've tried to protect your mother. You know, she herself was responsible for getting into these situations. Actually, all you should worry about now, is yourself".

He told me that his name was Carl – what a strange coincidence! He offered me to stay at his place after he called the police station to see if I was old enough to legally move out. At seventeen I was in the clear. Girls are allowed to move out at the age of sixteen, they explained.

Carl looked at me. "Now call home from here, and tell them". As I dialed our number I feared the worst. "Pedro?" I asked timidly. "I'm not coming home!" "OK". "Did you hear what I said? I'm not coming home!"

"Yeah, I know". Pedro hung up. He must have been mad, I thought. Pedro doesn't give away his temper at first, just sort of boils for a while. I was relieved, but still worried about Mom. I called back and asked how she was. When I heard her in the background, I felt better.

Carl sent out for a pizza and tried to make me feel at home. He told me that until I had enough money to rent a room somewhere, and until I had rested from this latest crisis, I was welcome to stay with him. His offer to help me was from his heart, not from the mind. I was very grateful feeling like a mistreated puppy who craved affection.

But when he told me that he was physically attracted to me, I explained that I was engaged to be married. He looked a little dejected but agreed it would be too difficult to live together. So after a few weeks I went out to find a room. I could not afford much because I had to pay for my doctor bills, too. My apartment was a single room in a rundown, cheap, ugly section of Chicago. It had a small bed, a refrigerator, and a table, and that was about all. The shower and toilets were down the hall, to be shared. The floor itself was a mess; drunks from the street slept there. Sometimes when I came home from work, I had to step over passed-out drunks in the hall.

The room cost me only about five dollars a week because I shared it with a guy named Roger. He slept there while I was at work, and I slept there while he worked. We hardly ever met each other.

With the doctor bills coming in, I was not doing very well financially. For quite some time now I had done very little modeling, and I regretted having spent my money so foolishly. Oh, how I could use it now. To help pay the bills I saw no other choice but to pawn my ring, but only for fifty dollars so I could later get it back. It turned out that I was not old enough, so I asked Roger to sign for me.

In my letters to Carl I persisted with the same lie about Mom being pregnant, for lack of knowing what to do. I had given a change-of-address notice to the post office.

One day a man stopped me on the street, while I was walking along in a little blue Indian costume, pants and a top, with my hair in pigtails. "You know, I'd love to take some pictures of you 'cause I do photography for Vogue. And if you let me do some photographs of you I'll give you lots of money." His name was Lonnie. He seemed like a rather nice guy.

"Well, all right, I do need the money", I responded. At his apartment I was really shy about taking off my clothes, so he took some photos of me in my Indian costume. I guess he was trying to butter me up when he took me to Carson's and bought a whole new outfit for me. With $ 25 I went to the beauty parlor, so that we could do some shots later on the lake front. I was thrilled out of my boots!

Returning to the apartment with me, Lonnie insisted again that I pose nude. I was too shy to do it, but I did strip down to my panties and bra, and he continued taking shots. Finally he did talk me into it and took some shots of me standing nude behind the frosted shower glass, with light pouring through from the back. They were all very modest poses, none of which I ever saw developed. Although Lonnie would not admit it, I suspected he had sold them to a slick magazine. Whenever I went to pose for him, Lonnie paid me $ 50, sometimes $ 75. The day finally came that he wanted to make love to me. I refused.

Lonnie asked me to be his girl. He offered to set me up in a beautiful apartment, he did not care that I was pregnant. I was afraid. When he fell asleep one day during work, I took three twenties from his wallet and left. Lonnie's wallet was packed with cash! He probably never realized anything was missing, and I did not feel the least bit guilty about it. I never saw him again.

I learned from this experience that here on Earth, where money is needed to survive, for a person in need it is very difficult not to fall into a trap of the negative forces.

I still worried a lot about my mother, so one day I daringly took a walk down into the neighborhood of the shop. Then I saw Mom across the street walking toward the barbershop with shopping bag in hand. My heart leaped in this moment of surprise; quickly I ducked into the entranceway of a store, watching as she passed. She looked bad, so worried and worn. It was all I could do to restrain myself from running to her and throwing my arms around her. I watched her with tears in my eyes until she was out of sight. Leaning against the building I cried. I loved her so much. How awful for her to suffer and not even understand Karma. I had never been able to talk to her about spiritual matters. When was I going to be with her again? Feeling terribly lonely that night, I fell asleep.

Not far from my house was a combination bowling alley and restaurant. On a hunch I stopped in to ask if they needed a waitress; they did, and the next day I started working there. A few days later my agent called with good news. I was offered a modeling job. Being almost six months pregnant there was hardly anything to be seen. It seemed that my life was making a turn for the better.

Returning home one day to get ready for the new work, I was shocked senseless. Pedro and Mom were there. "Oh God, what am I going to do?" I thought, quite shaken. "You are coming home with us", Pedro commanded, flashing a gun. "OK". What else could I say?! "How did you find out where I was?" I asked both of them. "Never mind, just get your clothes together", said Pedro.

Back at the barbershop they told me they wanted the baby, and they did not want anything to happen to it. That is why they were taking me home, to make sure I was all right and to pay all the hospital bills. I could not survive on my own, they reasoned. I realized that if I kept the baby I would need a babysitter while I worked. So at least with them I would know where it was, and it would have a full-time mother.

"Well, I have to go get my ring out of pawn. Can I go and at least do that?" But they would not let me out of their sight, not for five minutes. Together we went to retrieve the ring. It was gone! Stolen! Roger, my roommate, who had signed for me, apparently had gone back to enrich himself at my expense. Shattered, I realized that this was my reward for trusting people.

Pedro and Mom made me a virtual prisoner, especially after they had allowed me to go to the store on my own one day. I sneaked into a phone booth and called the police. "Can I talk to someone, because I've been raped and I'm pregnant, and they're locking me in the back of the house, and I want some help". They went through all the rigma-role of legality, and switching me from one person to another, when all of a sudden Pedro and Mom showed up to collar me and drag me back home. From then on I could not go anywhere unless I was with them.

Once again I broke the news to Mom that I was planning to turn Pedro over to the police. It certainly would take care of my fear of him. My mother begged and pleaded for me not to do it, that Pedro did not know what he was doing, and she loved him. Softheartedly I promised her once again – I would not send Pedro to jail.

I wrote to Carl and told him what was happening, the truth about Pedro raping me. I could no longer go on lying to him, and I desperately needed his help to get me out of here as he had promised. Carl never answered my letter. I wrote another and another, and I still did not get an answer. One day, I saw that a letter from Germany had arrived, but Mom would not let me read it. Mom finally explained that Pedro had thrown away all the others. She only found out just before this one arrived and wouldn't let him have it. I opened it to find that after my last desperate letter telling him the whole true story he had written several times, worried about me, wanting me to come to Germany right after the baby. Then when he did not hear from me for two months had married some woman with two children from a previous marriage. So that was that. He now was someone else's husband. I couldn't stop crying. "Why is it that every time I love somebody they either disappear or run out on me, or leave me? Why do I always have to go through this again? Why is everything snatched away from me when I am just about to get what I want, what I need ..." I suffered for a long time and once again, I was completely confused.

During the last months of my pregnancy, it was a rare thing for me to go anywhere at all. It was hell to be in the back of the barbershop all day – seemed as if my life with C.L. had begun all over again, only he looked different.

I spent the time thinking of my wonderful childhood and my decision that had brought me here. Karma is just a word; the suffering is not insinuated by those few letters. I had no choice but to accept and try to understand all that was happening.

One night, when I couldn't sleep, I asked Uncle Odin if he thought I had made the right decision choosing this life. His answer was that only I could make the decisions that guided my life. That I should never blame the child because of the consciousness of the father. I knew this was true. The child and the Soul were innocent of any circumstances before its arrival. It only chose to come out of a past connection to one or both of us.

I knew Mom really wanted another child. If I gave her this baby, I thought, I could make up for some of the suffering. And having the baby to care for, she would give up her drinking, I hoped.

Pedro and Mom went with me whenever I visited the doctor. The doctor was puzzled about me. He insisted I would not have the baby until December.

"No", I disagreed, "the baby will be born November the 18th and it will be a boy".

"Well, honey, how do you know this?" No woman had ever told him when her baby would be born. Should I tell him that I was communicating with the child? Nobody would believe me. So I said: "I just know ... and there is a streak of hair growing on my stomach". "What?" "A streak of hair on my stomach".

"And that's why you think it's a boy?" he asked, completely baffled.

"Well, yes, it has to do with hormones", I replied. "I never thought of that theory. Where did you get that from?" "Well, I don't know". What else could I say? The doctor was really kind to me. He treated me like I was a baby myself. I liked him.

"Sheila, one thing I do know. You're not going to have that baby until December.

Look at you, you're so tiny! How can you expect to have a baby that soon?" I did not argue with him anymore. Time will tell, I thought.

My attention turned to the baby and that I would have to give it up. This little being inside of me was part of myself. He could feel my emotions and sense how much I suffered. Yet how could I make him understand that I had to give him up? How was he going to feel about it later on? I had no idea how to solve this problem.

On the other hand, I could hardly wait for my freedom, for as soon as the baby was born I would leave the barbershop forever. Presently I was looking forward to having the baby, so I would be over with it and get out.

Freddie, the shoe-shine boy working at the barbershop, came to my rescue. Pedro apparently liked the little fellow so much that I was allowed to take him to a show. I was so happy to escape my prison for a few hours. Even better, his older brother Ronald met us there at the theater, and we fell for each other immediately. Freddie had talked about me at home, and Ronald of course felt very sympathetic. I learned later from Freddie that Ronald adored me even though I was getting fat in the tummy.

I started seeing Ronald quite often, whenever I could sneak away, which was when Pedro and Mom were passed out drunk. We planned for the future: as soon as I had the baby, we would move in together and be married later on. Desperate for affection, I secretly called Ronald whenever I could from the shop while Freddie watched for Pedro.

Finally, it was November and I started counting the days.

In the morning of November 16, my water broke and I called the kind doctor.

"Sheila; call a cab and come over to the hospital", he instructed. Mom had already gone off to work earlier. Pedro was busy at the barbershop. So I went to the hospital by myself, so sad and lonely in the cab, with my little suitcase. I was scared. This was my first baby and I did not know anything about having a baby. I wished I had called Mom; I knew Pedro would not tell her the news until she returned home from work.

At the hospital they put me to bed, prepped me, and started checking my dilation. I was not dilating and the pains were terrible. In the night they came to prop a pillow between my legs, to stop some of the pain, but in spite of all the pain pills it was just constant. The baby was pushing and bearing down, yet I was not dilating. "If we cannot dilate you artificially, we will have to do a caesarian", the doctor said. "But you should be able to have a baby normally. This isn't a very big baby."

All along the doctor had been repeating himself: "I can't believe you're ready to have the baby. You're not supposed to have this baby until December".

Mom came to visit me in the labor room. She gave me a kiss and a hug, telling me not to worry, that she would be with me all the time if it were possible.

Only fathers were allowed in the labor room, but she talked the attendants into letting her stay one hour. She stood there letting me squeeze her hand whenever I had a pain.

It was November 18, after thirty-four hours of labor, that they pushed me into the delivery room. The doctor had dilated me artificially by giving me a shot inside the vagina, which hurt fiercely. All of a sudden everything down there was numb. Afterwards I did not feel much of anything.

They strapped my left arm down and put my other hand on a grip. My feet went into the stirrups. "All right, push", the doctor instructed, as I looked up into the mirror hanging above my head. And it was so easy. I just pushed and it was like going to the bathroom, and the baby was out. It was a five pound-two ounce little boy, so little, only eighteen inches long.

"Oh my God! What's that thing hanging out of me?" I exclaimed, seeing a long bluish cord. "What happens, do you have to push that back up in there? Where does it go?" I was frightened.

The doctor was laughing. "Sheila, really, don't you know anything? This is the umbilical cord that connects the baby to the placenta, and it comes out after the baby is born. I thought, every woman knew this". "No, it scared me. I thought something was wrong with me", I admitted.

I was rolled into another room. "You can see your baby now", the nurse said, and she actually gave him to me.

Oh, he was beautiful! Just a gorgeous little baby. He had huge, sad gray eyes, and fuzz all over his head. "He looks just like me", I thought. I could not believe that I had had a baby, that this thing was real, and it came from inside me! I almost fell out of bed looking at him and holding him, I was so weak.

My tears were falling on his little face as I said, "I love you more than anything, and I hope you can understand that I don't want to give you away, that I am not ruthless and cold, that I do love you and I want to keep you with all my heart. I do not have a choice because they paid for my hospital bill and I have to give you up for that. And I'm afraid of Pedro".

The nurse came in and took the baby away and I calmed down and fell asleep.

When they brought the babies around to be fed for the first time, I was so nervous that I dropped and broke the bottle. The nurse told me that if he started choking I was to hold him upside down and pat him, so that the mucous could come out. I was horrified at the idea of actually doing it, but after the first and second time it was not so bad.

Mom came to visit me with a huge basket of fruit. She had seen the baby, she told me, and he was so beautiful, so lovely. As I lay there in bed, enjoying Mom's company, I realized that my deep love for her stemmed from many lifetimes of close relationships. Of all the people in my Earth life, she was most special, most dear to me.

When Pedro arrived, my mood changed. "Are you going to breastfeed the baby?" he asked. "No, I'm not", I replied. "I'm not going to stay around that long. I'm not going to live with you and nurse the baby. I want to leave". But first I had to go back to the barbershop with them. The ride home was trouble; my stitches hurt so badly. I could not get into a comfortable position and had to sit on my hands.

I had to lie down on my back or stand up; I could not sit down for the whole first week, unless I was soaking in hot water. The pain in my breasts intensified. I tried wrapping towels around my breasts to stop the milk, and I thought I would never get over the misery of the pain, my stitches hurting, milk dripping all over the place, the baby crying continuously.

Mom was at work and Pedro was busy cutting people's hair, so I was alone with the baby. It was just driving me crazy. I'd go to change his diaper, and I'd bend over and my milk would drip all over him, and he would pee on himself, and then he'd cry, and then he'd spit up, and then he'd cry, and then he'd spit up; and then I had to change the diaper again. I'd straighten up and he would cry again, and I'd check him and he was wet again, and my milk was just drip, drip, dripping.

So finally I started crying too, because my stitches were hurting and the baby would not leave me alone. I didn't know what to do. This very moment Mom came home from work. She and Pedro walked into the room just then and burst out laughing, which really got me mad. Here I was in pain, and they were laughing.

Mom took the baby and ran a bath of hot water for me, so that I could relax. I was never going to have another baby, I told Mom. I did not realize it was so miserable – milk dripping all over, stitches hurting, the baby screaming ... and never satisfied. Never in my life did I realize that a mother has to get up in the morning with the baby, and sometimes he cries at five o'clock. If he gets a bellyache or the hiccups at night, you have to walk the floor with him, feed him the bottle, and oh, the misery of having to do all this, hurting and being tired to the bones.

At nights, with the least little sound from him I'd be sitting straight up in bed: I would see his little eyes shining in the dark; he would be jerking around instead of sleeping. Of course he was a cute little baby, and being mine he was the most beautiful baby in the world. We called him JoJo, but his real name was José Guadalupe Francesco Garcia Mora.

Mom and Pedro were proud of him; they took him all over the neighborhood. I was proud, too, but I could not tell anybody. One night when they went out to dinner, I wrapped JoJo real warm and ran as fast as I could through the ice and snow, all the way to Ronald's house so his parents could see the boy. I was so proud, and everybody was dishing out compliments. But I had to hurry back home.

I told Ronald that I would be moving in with him pretty soon, and that we could get married in no time. I had never really thought about being in love with Ronald. It was just that I liked him very much, and he was kind and sweet and gentle to me. I figured that if he liked me when I was pregnant, he would like me when I was not. The problem was that most of our relationship had developed over the phone, at a time when I was desperately lonely.

JoJo was six weeks old when I finally left the barbershop. What a relief! But by moving out of the house, I was exchanging one set of problems for another. Pedro and Mom did not make a fuss when I left. I just got ready, collected my clothes, and walked the six blocks to Ronald's house. But I very quickly found out that by moving in with him I hadn't found a free life but only a set of new problems.

Even though the one-bedroom apartment was a nice place, I figured that the rent we were paying was too high. Cooking for Ronald was boring, but I never said much about it because I disliked arguments. Hamburger meat was fine any way I prepared it, or spaghetti. But there were hardly any vegetables he liked, and I was not allowed to experiment with meals. Ronald did not like beef stew, did not like fish, did not like shrimp, did not like anything, it seemed to me. He also liked to play cards, which I had never played in my life. That is how he spent his evenings, playing cards and drinking beer with the people on the second floor. It wasn't my kind of life, but I tried to go along with it because I thought I was in love with him, and I didn't know the kind of person he was. Ronald was insecure. Every time I turned around, he was saying: "I love you. Do you love me?" It was always: "Do you love me?"

It bothered me that he insisted on going out with an old girlfriend. He was talking about her all the time. It hurt me to see how insincere or perhaps immature he was. Ronald and I argued heatedly about it when I blamed him for being childish. If he was to marry me he had to stop playing his games.

Then he started picking on me, about my earrings, my makeup, my clothes, the way I behaved. At a Christmas party with his family I danced with his mother just for fun, and Ronald reprimanded me for it. "Well this is silly", I thought, disgusted. "What the hell is he going to do if I dance with someone else?" I started seeing through our whole relationship.

Day after day we argued more and more over little things, and we practically lived at his parents' home. Both his mother and father drank, which reminded me too much of the existence I had just left. I realized that I had been hasty in moving in with Ronald; since I had been so eager to get away from Mom and Pedro, I had failed to do much thinking. My desperation made me think that this would be my way out. During the time that I had been locked up in the barbershop, Ronald was the only boy my age who I was able to see and talk to. Therefore, what I felt as love was really only my infatuation with the idea of getting away. I talked myself into thinking that I loved him, when I really did not much know about him. Many people get into the same unfortunate mess.

Ronald had been drafted and when he went away for basic training, I moved in with a girl I had met at work. My decision was made; I intended to break up with him but I did not know exactly how to do it.

One night he picked me up at the restaurant where I worked. He talked about his plans for us till late at night. He wanted me to move down to Florida, where he was going to be based. And he still planned to go out with his old girlfriend, who lived there. This really peeved me. “I really don’t love this man”, I said to myself once more, “and I’m not going to stay with him.” When he finally fell asleep, I got up to write him a note: “I’m sorry, Ronald; I haven’t been true to you while you were away. I realize now that my moving in with you was just an escape, and at the time you were the only person who was kind to me. I thank you for that, but I’m sorry, I don’t think we can make a life together. Apparently you are still in love with this girl in Florida, and I just don’t think that I’m right for you. Goodbye”.

Outside I walked the streets, all over the neighborhood. I knew that as soon as Ronald woke up and read the note, he would drive over to his parents’ house with the news. When I finally did see his car go by, I said to myself, “Well, it’s all over. Now I can go home”.

But just about closing time the next night, I saw Ronald and his father standing outside the restaurant, waiting for me. My coworkers were excitedly waiting for something dramatic to happen, while I fidgeted and delayed going home.

“Sheila, I’m not going to let you get away with this!” Ronald began. Then his father spoke up. “Look, you’ve made a commitment to our son, and you’re going with him”.

Ignoring his father, I turned to Ronald. "You can't make me go with you, and you really don't want me to, because I don't love you. You can't make someone love you".

"And speaking of commitments", I said looking at his father, "Ronald didn't make any commitments to me. I don't even have an engagement ring, and what about that girl in Florida he insists on dating?"

Meanwhile, Ronald's father resorted to calling me names. Ronald interrupted him, saying, "I think you should stay out of it". "Well, we want our TV set back", Ronald's father demanded. I was using their TV set in my apartment.

"Here is the key", I instructed. "Go and take the TV and leave the key with the landlady in the lobby, and I'll pick it up when I get there". The two of them just glared at me, then left. I never saw them again.

Image 6: Omnec in her wedding dress (for her wedding to Carl) at Pedro's barbershop in Chicago. She is 5 months pregnant with JoJo.

Image 7: Omnec and lil Joe.

Image 8: Donna with Jay, who adopted JoJo.

Chapter 5 – Renewed Confidence

It happened during a stay with my grandmother in Tennessee. Mom and I had taken the baby to the south where we proudly presented JoJo to the family. No one doubted that he was Mom's son.

Suddenly I received an inner message from my people. It was urgent. I was to go to Nevada immediately. I didn't tell anybody, but sent Mom and the baby back to Chicago with an excuse. Then I took the next bus and travelled across the American continent once again.

Two days later I arrived at Boulder City, at about two in the afternoon. I checked into a hotel, took a shower, and changed clothes. Downstairs in the lobby I saw that this hotel was the perfect starting point for bus tours to Boulder Dam. Again the inner message, the inner urging was clear. I was to take the next bus to Boulder Dam, where I would be met by one of our people.

My next moves became clear with every step of the way. At the Dam I decided not to finish the rest of the tour. Instead, I entered the coffee and souvenir shop and sat down at the counter. I ordered a glass of Coke. A man got up from one of the booths and walked to the cash register. Right away he stood out from the other people, just the way he looked, his face. I could tell he was a Martian. I looked at him and he looked at me, and we knew. I paid for my Coke and followed him outside, neither of us saying a word. In silence the Martian unlocked the door and we both got into his car. He knew my name: "Omnec, I am Flynn. I live in Las Vegas and I have a business there. I was contacted by your uncle."

He said, "I was to bring you to a certain place, and he said you would be here at the Dam somewhere. I looked for you and I knew you immediately, from his description", the man from Mars continued.

I told him I lived in Chicago with a family, and that I had been raised by a family there. I was going to meet my uncle because there was some reason for my living on Earth that I had to learn about, other than what I knew already. He just smiled at me, said he thought he knew what it was all about.

"It seems everyone except myself knows", I thought. The Martian laughed: "Perhaps they do." Startled, I remembered that our people communicate mentally. "Sheila is the name I use here", I continued. "Omnec Onec is my full name, and it means spiritual rebound. I have been told that it is to be used only after I start my spiritual work by those who know where I come from.

We drove to a place in the desert close to the Arizona border. For an hour or so we rode slowly along a bumpy desert road. Sometimes it seemed to disappear into the rubble, but my companion apparently knew where he was going. It surely was wonderful to be in the presence of someone with a higher consciousness for a change. I took advantage of this and relaxed to soak it up.

Our destination was deep among the hills and valleys of the desert, in an area of huge cliffs, hills and boulders. The sun was already setting when we parked the car where the road finally ended. Flynn led the way to a secluded area surrounded on three sides by steep hills. My heart was pounding madly. Suddenly I saw a silvery spaceship sitting in the dusk ahead of us. Except for the lights that poured out through the port-holes, it was dark. The ramp was down and several figures stood there with flashlights. I recognized my uncle immediately, even though I could not see his face. I ran over into his arms. He smiled at me. We stood there motionless with our arms around each other. I soaked in the warmth and love I felt from being with him again.

Odin motioned to his friends that we would enter the ship alone, together with the pilot. I gave the space greeting of passing the right hand clockwise over the heart, then clasping hands while looking deeply into each other's eyes, nodding. The men went off toward the car while Odin and I entered the ship. The ramp slid back in and the round opening closed behind us. I was excited, just touching and looking at everything, walking around. But Uncle Odin asked me to sit down on the curved seats around the floor lens. Looking down through the lens I could see lights of cars on the highway, traveling back and forth, the Dam below in the distance, all lit up. What a sight, this huge Dam sitting in the rocks and bathed in bright lights. There is nothing quite like Las Vegas at night, because of all the bright lights. From the air it was even more beautiful and spectacular, all those lights spread out below and surrounded completely by the darkness of the desert.

To my surprise I hadn't noticed that the ship had taken off. Having been out of these ships for such a long time and so full of joy about my reunion with Odin, I had forgotten the peculiar lack of feeling any movement. The craft itself was similar to the ships of our previous trips. Again there was the slight humming sound, and the soft light that filled the interior but came from no one source. There were no shadows.

Odin told me about how my father had not wanted to be left behind on the Astral Plane when Aunt Arena also manifested her physical body. He was now living with them on one of the big mother ships and they were working on their invention together. My father was very ill; the physical world did not agree with him. Arena was taking care of him. It seemed that my father's present incarnation was about over.

He reminded me that I could not tell people about this trip when I returned to Chicago, no matter how much I wanted to.

"Omnec, my child, you have had much suffering." I raised my head to look into his calm eyes, feeling so sad because I was trapped in my own suffering, the same suffering I had treated others to in my past lives. With his words came a feeling within me of wanting to cry and bury my face in his warmth and strength of his being, but also the feeling of joy to know I was not suffering for nothing, and realizing that somewhere in the world every day, people were experiencing the same pains as I had experienced.

He continued. "Yes, the deep light of burning compassion and sadness rests in your eyes. But with it comes the look of wisdom and mystery for those who knowest not these feelings. I would gladly take your suffering if it were not a lesson for you as Soul! Don`t ever think we have forgotten you. You are special. Even though it was very painful for us it was all we could do, Arena and I, not to interfere and take you away from all the suffering because of our love for you. And yet, we were warned many times by the Masters not to do this, no matter how much you suffered, because then you would not have these experiences and grow.

But we never did forsake or forget you. You had our love and support all along, and were in our hearts and thoughts always. And we were with you spiritually".

It hit a soft spot in my heart to hear this. Tears were in my eyes as he spoke, and of course tears were in his eyes, too. This made me feel that my suffering was not in vain, and I realized that my suffering must have a meaning. If my uncle and aunt had to let me suffer, then they themselves suffered.

Uncle Odin confirmed my feelings. "Through your sufferings we have learned a great deal of compassion ourselves, through watching you and feeling the agony you were going through. I know that many times you must have felt as if you had been completely neglected, but this is not true. It is very difficult to be able to contact you because of where you are living, and because I'm not prepared to live in that kind of society. It takes an unearthly amount of courage and stamina to be able to live on Earth. Some people make the choice and live here comfortably. Others cannot. I never made that choice because I did not feel that I could".

Uncle Odin then began to speak about my special mission on Earth, which the Masters of Retz had hinted at. In the future I would make myself known by writing a book; this had been foreseen. But of course it would be my own choice. The choice would be made based on a great spiritual teacher whom I would meet. The spiritual Master was someone I had known very well in past lives, and whom I had seen as a child. My uncle predicted that very soon I would find the spiritual teachings I had known on Venus as a child. Right now at the time he was telling me this, the man whom I had seen as a child was translating these teachings into the English language and bringing them to the American people. From America the teachings would be spread to other parts of the world. I was not to search for him; that would be a mistake and would lead me astray. I would meet him naturally in my life.

The book, he went on to explain, would be a good way of introducing people from other planets, because I was unique in coming here as a child and living among the people. As of this day, Odin added, no one had written a book of this sort – a first-hand account by an individual from another planet. I would be the living proof of my story. The Brotherhood of the Planets had tried in many ways to make their existence known, little by little. But the truth had always been covered up.

I wondered about this. "How can I prove anything? I look like many other people on Earth". Uncle Odin smiled. "Do not be mistaken, my child. There is something very unusual and different about you, a feeling if nothing else. But most people will see something unusual about you". I hesitated to believe this, mostly because from living on Earth so long I figured I had grown to be like everyone else. "You are not like everyone else, Omnec", he continued responding to my thoughts. "Think of yourself as different and special, and in this way you will keep that specialness which you do have."

"Because you are here, you have the opportunity to write about your life, and your book will come out at the right time. It will be for the good of the people, to give people hope for their world, their Earth. And then some day Earth can be a part of the Brotherhood of the Planets".

By relating every experience I had had on Earth, people would be able to relate to my suffering, to how I had lived. The reason I had been put through so many different experiences was not always Karma, but also so that I would have a great number of different Earth experiences.

In the future I would not always be living the best, I would not always have the money or all the things I needed. But I would never do without, even though I might often get by with very little. Life would be better to me when I was older, and I was to remember that the teachings were coming. My uncle did not know the name under which they would appear; it depended on the Master who was bringing them into the open.

There was not much time he could spend with me. It was almost time for us to say goodbye, and before I knew it we had already returned to the spot. "How quickly time goes when you are with someone you love, and how slowly, Uncle, when you are in pain", I said. "Isn't there any way you could come with me? I know I'm being selfish, but I crave affection and understanding. I feel so strange with people to whom I really cannot communicate. It was so wonderful to see you again", I went on. "Thank you for taking the time and effort to tell me these things. All of it gave me new courage".

Uncle Odin nodded. "I know that your life will change. And I heard about the child that you have. I do know many things that have happened to you, even though you cannot see or hear me. I will let you know, somehow, if your father translates."

We landed and it was time for the examination of my physical functions and to balance any negative effects on my mental and emotional health. I undressed and was provided with a special light robe. The temperature on board of the craft is always comfortable as everything automatically responds to your needs. Meanwhile I went into a deep meditation and fell asleep.

Certain energies are directed by thought through a large crystal and several small ones that are lowered by automation over certain locations of the body and change positions as needed. They can also harmonize and balance the grid lines and chakra system. They also use special harmonic sounds in combination with the crystal energy for healing.

When I awoke after about an hour, I felt renewed and glowing as I re-dressed. I had a very nice fruit drink with Odin, while he explained that now he could communicate with me telepathically without interference from any location. Up to this time, energy and thoughts from other people around me had created difficulties.

The door opened, and we stepped outside together. With hands clasped together we stood there, facing each other. He gave me a light embrace and I kissed him. Odin looked deeply into my eyes. "Keep courage in everything that happens, and if you find yourself getting depressed, it is very normal. You have more strength than many people, and do not forget that you are special. And no matter what anyone says, or how you are treated, do not hold it against them. They do not know any better".

He kissed me on my forehead and walked away. That was it. Everyone said goodbye at the car, and as Flynn, my driver, backed off and turned around I could see my uncle waving in the headlights. I kept looking out the back window and waving until there was nothing more to be seen, not even a speck. A spark of light rose into the sky; until it was out of sight I watched. For a while I did not say a word, wishing I were leaving in it.

I turned to Flynn. "Thank you very much for bringing me out here. I appreciate it very much. It meant a great deal to me". He replied, and it was a pleasure to meet me. He felt it was an honor, and that it was his part in the whole movement to make man recognize his ancestors from outer space. He drove me back to the hotel, where we said goodbye.

On the way back to Chicago, I relived those special moments over and over in my mind. How wonderful to see Uncle Odin again, to have another memory of my people to cling to and to carry me through many more troubles I was to face, to once again have the reassurance of what I am striving for here, and to know how wonderful human beings can be. How exciting it would be to find my spiritual teachings. I wished I could talk about it to somebody.

But now I had to go back and continue my life as if nothing had happened. I felt that I would burst, with all this locked inside. Surely my expression, when I looked into the mirror, was much different than it had been before. The defeated look was gone and my eyes sparkled with confidence.

The chain of events that changed my whole life, as my uncle had prophesied, began when I met a girl named Margie. We had worked together before and we became friends now, also spending our free time together. From the way she talked, it seemed to me that Margie`s second home was Oldtown. This was the area of Chicago where all the hippies lived and had fun. I had never seen hippies before and I did not know what they were. In fact, I did not have much of an idea what was going on the world. I did not know about the Vietnamese war, or LSD, or any of these things.

My mother had once tried to tell me about drugs, and all of these contemporary problems. She was very much in touch with what was going on, but I really did not care. It would go in one ear and out the other. As a result, I mistakenly believed that the drug LSD was a group of people.

I went to work at a restaurant and I went home, and I went out with my friends. That was my life. I never watched television, never read the newspapers, and I couldn't care less for the radio. The only entertainment I had at home were the records I played and the gothic novels I occasionally read.

Margie was always trying to tell me about the be-ins and love-ins, and all the great things they had in Oldtown. She wouldn't let me be, until I agreed to go with her one day. So the night came when she and her boyfriend picked me up after work. In Oldtown I noticed that a lot of people had beards and long hair, and I already knew that this was the style in bands and singing groups. To me it was very acceptable. It was fine, if that was the way they wanted to look. I did not think of them as being different. On Venus we accept people as they are and respect their appearance and clothing as a part of the personality.

That evening I wore my cowgirl outfit from Nevada – tight jeans, boots, cowboy jacket, and cowboy hat. I was always dressing in a special way, but it did not seem strange to me; it was just the way I felt like dressing. And only in Oldtown did I feel the least self-conscious. It was exciting. I was most impressed by the fact that I could be free there; I could dress the way I wanted to, and I wasn't ridiculed. Instead, people in Oldtown seemed to appreciate strange ways of dressing.

I first saw him while we were trying to find a parking spot. "Look at that guy, Margie", I exclaimed, pointing ahead. "He looks like he must be a dancer, the way he walks". Right away I had noticed him, walking across the street in a big black cape, looking strikingly like

Hercules with his bushy hair and beard. And he was so tall, walked so gracefully that I was sure he was a dancer. For some unexplained reason I was attracted to this man. I just had a strong feeling that I would one day know him, but when? Deep inside I sensed the unmistakable presence of destiny.

I still carried the toy airgun which I had found laying on the sidewalk after I had stopped by my apartment to change clothes. This plastic thing made a hell of a noise but I was happy as a child playing with my new toy.

Being impulsive and loving to watch people react, I began to shoot at the people with my air rifle, and they would pretend falling dead on the sidewalk! That was fun. Everybody seemed to make a big game of it. It was common to have street theater.

As the time went on, I grew bolder and bolder. When I shot at a cab driver, he yelled out the window: “What is this, open season on cab drivers?” It was thrilling yet unusual to see how friendly everyone was. But what I did not know was that they were all wrapped up in the Vietnamese war and the hippie/police conflict. I just intended it as a joke.

Then I pointed at a police car and shot. That was a mistake. In an instant they had pulled over and jumped out. Asking my name they pulled the gun from me, checking it out, then returned it. What could they do? It was just a toy gun.

“If I were you, I wouldn’t point that at policemen”, the officer warned.

“Why?” I did not know that the hippies and the police had been battling. They must have thought I was just a smart disrespectful hippie girl.

Margie and I invented a game where I would chase her down the street, screaming, “You no-good son of a bitch! I’ll get you for that!” And we would stop right in front of a restaurant with a big plate glass window, where I would shoot her dead on the side-walk.

Margie was really a fantastic actress. She could scream with pain and stagger to the ground so realistically that the people would come running out every single time to see what had happened. Then, of course, she would jump up laughing. The police would appear, too. We were having so much fun, we did not think of the shock that we created.

Margie and I were just leaving one of the alleys in Old-town lined with small shops, when the intriguing guy in the black cape walked right past me down the sidewalk. I recognized him immediately.

He was not like all the others, for when I shot at him he just kept walking.

Then I got an idea. I ducked into an alley way and shot at him as he passed. He ignored us! “Hey” I called, “I shot you!” He stopped and turned around. “Why didn’t you react?” I asked. “I don’t believe in violence” he said. “Well, neither do I” I defended myself. “It is only a toy!” – “It represents the real item” he replied. “Well, I am sorry if I offended you” I apologized. “Don’t worry” he said. “Would you come to join me for tea?” he asked. I said “yes, thank you” knowing I had never drank tea except in Tibet!

He said his name was Stanley. He lived nearby. He explained that his family was Jewish but atheist, not believing in God. I told him about my family and where I worked. We parted and he said he would come for coffee where I worked.

Stan was also surprised to see his cousin Kenny was there. I knew Kenny. He came in often and had just asked me out when Stan came in! How interesting, I knew Stan’s cousin first, but he had asked me out the very night I had a date with Stan! There must be some connection to this family! Only time would tell.

He was very interested in my ideas because they were unusual, not college-born, so we had an attraction for each other right away. Together we walked to my apartment.

I unlocked the door and flipped on the lights. Stan just stood there, staring. I did not realize I almost threw him into a state of shock because he had been smoking marijuana earlier. I had never taken drugs before and did not have any friend who did – my consciousness just was not there. But I suppose it just blew his mind, as they say, to see the flashing lights in my apartment.

Overhead were red and blue blinking lights, over in the corner was a yellow blinking light, and on the shelf was a little blinking light box. The yellow light was from one of those street barricades. A few weeks ago I had dragged it up the stairs, fearful of being caught in the act. But I liked it so much that I felt it just belonged in my apartment.

Stan could not believe it, the combination of all those lights, I suppose it had a powerful effect on him, because he just stared through the doorway for awhile. Then he laughed. "What's so funny?" "Oh, nothing", he said, chuckling, "I just couldn't believe you were the type to have these kinds of lights and everything". I was perplexed. "What do you mean, the type?" "Well, I`ll explain it to you later. As a matter of fact, I`ve set up part of a collage at home, like a light machine. I`ll have to show it to you sometime." "Yes, that sounds interesting. What's a light machine?" "Well, it`s just a combination of lights and different things that makes patterns, that throws different patterns out and makes nice designs and colors". "That`s interesting. I`d like that". Stan glanced around. "Look at your place. You almost have it yourself. It just blew my mind".

Returning from the bathroom, I was just shocked speechless, as if I had been hit by a ton of bricks. I did not know what to do. Lying on my couch bed, which I hadn't bothered to make up, was Stan ... stark naked! Big six-foot-four Stan was all sprawled out completely naked and looking very much at ease, and not hiding what he really wanted.

I was used to the standard procedure of boys taking me to dinner, or taking me places, and buttering me up before they would try to make a pass at me. Stan was just so honest that it shocked me. Even though I had had many boyfriends and was not an inexperienced girl, I was still a little prudish. I was reluctant to undress. It may sound strange, but that's the way it was and still is.

When I saw Stan stretched out on the bed like that, I did not know whether to run, or to act like I hadn't seen anything, or what. I did not want to embarrass him, or act like I was shocked, because I was the one who invited him up to the apartment; and whatever happened was my own fault, my own consequence. This is how I felt at that time.

I acted as if this was an everyday thing. I took off my clothes down to bra and panties and sat down on the side of the bed. I tried to be casual and cool.

I talked to Stanley as if he was my long-lost brother, telling him all about my baby, and the rough life I had had with C.L. and Pedro. I know that this sounds strange, to tell a stranger all of this. But somehow I felt that Stan and I belonged together. I just knew it. I wanted honesty between us; I wanted him to know all about me, so that right there in the beginning he could make up his mind. I did not want to give him the impression that I was something I really was not. Later the truth would be harder to tell. So I sat there and told him all about coming here when I was seven, and some of the highlights of my life here and on Venus. I was sitting there in my underwear telling him all these things until five in the morning! I was talking, not knowing what else to do. All of a sudden he spoke up. "You talk too much", and pulled me into bed. I could hardly believe it, but Stanley turned out to be the first person I had ever relaxed with. He was so natural and free.

I had not had sexual relations with anyone willingly before Stan. I always felt that if I aroused a boyfriend then they should have some kind of release.

But Stan was different. I felt comfortable and safe, and I was not afraid of him. He was so gentle and so kind, and yet at the same time there was his strength.

Making love with him was beautiful, perhaps because he aroused me first, took the time to make me feel good. Most of my experience with boys had been meaningless, I realized, because they were always thinking only of themselves. Stan was considerate.

In a way, we both knew, even though it was the strangest feeling we had ever had, that we belonged together. And it was just love, real love. It was not a possessive love, and we just kept it that way. Two Souls having shared love during so many lifetimes before had come together again.

Image 9: Omnec and Stan, wedding.

Chapter 6 – The Girl from Venus

Before I met Stanley I had always searched for happiness, and when I had it and was about to clasp it to my bosom in gratitude, it was gone like sand dripping away through my fingers. In my whole life I had never really had the kind of love I wanted. This time I felt that our love was going to last.

I told Margie that Stanley and I were going to be married. Not knowing whether she would understand, I could not tell her we would just be living together, for at this time concubinage wasn't accepted socially.

The first night when Stanley surprised me by walking into the restaurant where I worked, people were shocked. They just were not prepared to see a hippie, with a big bush of hair and a beard, and a flower tucked behind his ear, and the way he dressed – all this just simply didn't match their concept of a tidy student.

These Jewish middle class people had neat categories for people, and Stanley fit into the hippie category. I had never felt that way. A beard, or however a person dressed never made any difference to me, because individuality was a part of our culture on Venus.

The people at the restaurant finally got used to Stanley, after seeing enough of his beads and long hair. But my mother never quite got over the shock. Every day she called to tell me how horrible Stanley was, that she could not stand him, that he was up to no good, and that he was going to ruin me. Part of her problem was that she feared I would start doing all these things she had read about, getting involved with heavy drugs.

My mother finally agreed to do me the favor of getting to know Stanley. We arranged to meet her the next time she took JoJo to the doctor, whose office happened to be a few blocks from our house. The meeting was a success! Was I surprised to see the two of them discovering all the interests they shared! Stanley was studying meditation at the time and told Donna all about it, even gave her a book on Maharishi Yoga. She on the other hand had been studying Rosicrucian teachings, so they really got to talking and I could tell that she liked him. Mom and Stanley got along very well.

The next day she called and told me just that, how much she liked him, and that she was terribly sorry about all the things she had said before. Now that she really knew him as a person, she found him to be a beautiful being. That made life a lot easier for me, too.

Very few people were living together seriously, as Stanley and I. Most of the hippies lived in groups and switched partners all the time, and some of them got hung up in drugs really badly. Stanley and I never got trapped in heavy drugs, mostly because I had flatly told him I would not stand for it.

One night, Stanley asked if I would like some pot. I did not know what that was, I told him. He explained marijuana, that people smoked it, and that it was not dangerous. I asked what acid was, and then I finally learned that LSD was not a group of people. Somehow, when he was explaining it, I had a strange feeling of fear and an inner message. I came right out with what I thought.

"Stanley, there's one thing you are going to have to promise me if we are going to live together, you won't take any more acid. I don't want to hold it over your head, I just want it out in the open now because I believe that it is dangerous for you, especially if you are an artist and a very sensitive person, I don`t think you should take it."

We talked it over and he wasn't too sure about it, but he sort of understood what I was trying to tell him. Stanley responded that I really didn't understand LSD. "Well, maybe I don't", I said, and we dropped it there.

I found out that smoking pot brought out the childlike quality lurking ever near the surface of man. And yet I did not care for it as much as I saw so many others care and ever depend on it. It was fun to get stoned at times, but I was careful not to get caught in the habit.

It disturbed me to have the world look distorted; I liked to be in control of myself. Smoking marijuana got us totally involved in the ordinary patterns and colors and things around us. Our attention was totally absorbed by what we were doing, and in that way we became children.

The one thing that bothered me about the hippie scene was their hang-up on war; they put too much attention on trying to change society. Trying to change the world did not make sense to me because I knew that the physical universe will always be a warring universe, being the lowest plane. And change always arises from the inner of man, not through changing the outer conditions.

Stanley lived in a little green stucco house. The place was awfully messy inside, but of course he was a bachelor and I did not expect much from him. I took it upon myself to clean up his house, which was really a mess. I was hoping he would not be offended, but Stanley liked the idea. A couple of hours later the apartment was looking neat: One room became our bedroom. I persuaded Stanley to move the top mattress of his bed there; the bottom part of the bed was our living room couch. Placing a table top upon a large, old trunk, and a truck seat and record player case at either end, our dining room set was complete. Stanley and I mutually decided that I would work while he stayed home to do his art. I would support the family until he got on his feet with his art. This was the pattern we started our lives with.

Up to this point I had never really understood abstract art, and I never tried to. But when Stanley started showing me his work and explained what it meant, it made sense, and it was truly beautiful.

I suppose that when you are in love with someone there is a difference, you will be interested in things that he is interested in. Stanley started dragging out his paintings, and I began to see things in them – love, hate, anger, joy, whatever he must have been feeling when he painted them. Even though there was nothing but colors, I could understand. Stanley began showing me a lot of the good things in life, cultural things that I had never been exposed to here on Earth. I learned that Stanley was a very well-read person, who enjoyed many forms of art and music, especially classical music and folk songs.

I found his habit of drinking herb tea delightful. After all these years of being subjected to the worst foods of the American people, I had to learn a good deal about good nutrition.

Stanley and I as well as the rest of the hippies in Old Town had very little sense of time. We thought nothing of staying out until five in the morning, walking around, visiting friends, going to the lake to see the sunrise. Practically every night we went to a nearby coffeehouse where all sorts of interesting and creative people from the neighborhood performed musically and poetically. Occasionally Stanley would have his art displayed here.

Before long, I had a reputation all over Old Town as the girl from Venus, and people seemed to be constantly taking me to introduce me to their friends. Stanley had told a couple of friends about me, and the word had seemed to spread overnight. In small groups I spoke about my life on Venus, but only when I was asked. The reactions were mixed – some of the hippies thought I was crazy, and others were very receptive, but even to be considered crazy was a cool thing for hippies.

One summer afternoon Stan and I came home and took a shower to cool off from the June heat. The strangest thing happened as we were starting to get dressed. I don't know how it happened, and neither one of us can remember how we ended up on our knees in the bathroom, facing each other.

Stanley broke the silence. "Sheila, do you know what's happening?"

"What?"

"This is our marriage ceremony."

"What do you mean?"

Stanley was smiling. "Don't you feel it?"

"Yeah, I really do feel something strange", I replied. How did we get on our knees?"

"I don't know."

Obviously, we had made a spiritual ceremony that seemed quite natural to both of us. It seemed to be destiny. We embraced. That evening both of us were in Old Town shopping for rings. Being very poor, we settled for two rings made of woven reeds. We realized that we could always get married later on, but the bond between us was so strong and meaningful that a piece of paper just didn't seem too important. Later Stanley realized that this day had been the summer solstice, the longest day of summer.

Stanley had called his parents and told them about me, he said, adding that he wanted me to meet them sometime soon.

Stanley's mother telephoned us and arranged to pick us up in the evening to take us to dinner at her house. I was a bit nervous about meeting Clara, but the fact that Stanley had already told her all about me made me feel more at ease.

Clara was a very attractive woman. She and Stanley had the same thick curling hair and deep-set eyes. Her square face showed strength of character, and a lot of smile lines and crinkles around the eyes suggested a keen sense of humor. She smiled a lot and was one to make a person at ease. However, she had a commanding air about her. I sensed that Clara was a very deep and personal woman. As she spoke, I could tell she was a brilliant woman, someone who expected honesty and admired strength. I liked her from the start.

The house was crowded with people, which was not unusual, Stanley explained. Clara and Hans's (his stepfather from Germany) house was always open; people were always running in and out. Clara was laughing about this. "Yes, I guess I'm young at heart." Everyone loudly agreed. It showed she was popular among the young people. Dinner was delicious. Clara and Hans were excellent hosts, and of course Clara asked one question after another – about myself and my family, but I did not mind answering because she did seem sincerely interested.

Clara's first impression of me may have been a little bewildering, because I had just returned from a modeling job and was wearing my leopard-print jumpsuit with big hoop earrings and a snake bracelet on my arm, sandals and my hair in pony tails.

Later in the evening Clara mentioned that I must be some kind of wild go-go dancer out to get her son. "Well Clara", I replied, "did you ever think that your son might be a little wild-looking too? You should hear how my mother feels about him." She laughed. "You don't think your own child is wild – you get used to him. And then they look wilder than anyone else. You know, he called me and said he was in love with you. For the first time in his life he was really in love. And I thought he was crazy, him being twenty-three and you only eighteen."

"I may be young, Clara, I said, "But I had to grow up awfully fast." As our conversation went on, I began to like Clara more and more. Just as I thought, she had a fantastic sense of humor and was very warm and outgoing.

Stanley had two younger siblings, brother and sister. The whole family was very closely knit, and of course very well-to-do because Hans owned a famous candy factory, Chris Candy. As a matter of fact, President Kennedy ordered Hans' chocolates for the White House because he loved their exquisite taste.

Later on when I met his uncles and aunts, I found out that I had been waiting on these people for months – they had been customers at the restaurant ever since I worked there. Here I had been nervous about meeting Stanley's relatives.

The only thing that bothered me about Stanley was that he smoked pot all the time. He was smoking his way through two or three nickel bags each week. I finally discovered to my dismay that nickel bags did not cost five cents each, but five dollars. That was mighty expensive on our slim budget. Stanley was relying more and more on the stuff to do his art and to make love.

Times got worse. I was supporting Stanley and working, which I did not mind doing, but the problem came up again that he began withdrawing into himself. Mostly it had to do with him not doing anything, it seemed to me.

It did get to be a bother because Stanley stopped responding to me; he wouldn't even talk to me, or make love. It was just as if I wasn't there, as if I didn't exist, and it drove me crazy. I was supporting him and I did want some love, I did want something in return for what I was giving him, even if it was just him talking to me.

The few times that he did make a go at painting, he would lock himself into the other room. He didn't want me around.

I figured that I could be closer to him if I started painting too, which I did, and I enjoyed it very much. But that didn't help Stanley; he just did not want to respond to anything. For hours he would just lie on the bed, silent. I spoke to Clara and found out that Stanley had a deep seated emotional problem and had been hospitalized for several months. It seemed to be a recurring problem.

Finally it became so disturbing that I could not take any more. It hurt me too much to be ignored. "Stanley, when you were sick before, your mother took you and put you in a hospital, had you taken care of like a child. But I'm not going to do that because I'm not your mother. I don't like this nonsense you're going through. It isn't necessary for you to act this way."

I flatly told Stanley I was leaving him. I didn't mind supporting him, but I did want some love, a person who responded to me. And I wasn't going to give out all my love to someone who gave nothing in return.

I threw my clothes into a suitcase and headed for the door. Finally he reacted. As I opened the door, he jumped up and grabbed me by the arm, slinging me back into the room. I landed on my behind.

"You're not going anywhere!" Stanley ordered. Then he sat down and started talking, which made me so happy that I didn't care about my bruised bottom.

"Well, perhaps you should get a job," I suggested.

"No, I'll start doing my paintings."

"OK, fine", I agreed. But it was not too long afterwards when fate decided Stanley would indeed have to go to work.

On a Saturday afternoon I got off the underground train close to home. Apparently I was the only one who got off at that stop. A huge black guy who looked almost like a football player raced down the stairs past me as I went up. Then I heard him running back up behind me, but I took no notice because it occurred to me that he may have forgotten to get a transfer pass. The next thing I knew was that a huge hand was over my mouth and another between my legs from behind, and I wasn't even touching the ground anymore! Words cannot describe the horrible feeling of deathly fright at moments like this. Instinctively I bit his hand. He smacked me violently and threw me to the cement landing. With one thundering kick into my ribs, he dashed up the stairs and out of the subway station.

Momentarily, a whole crowd of people made their way down the stairs, one of them a black policeman. "Stop that guy!" I said to him breathlessly. "He just attacked me." "I can't help you now. I have to go to work", he answered, continuing on his way to the trains. I was horrified! What kind of a job does he have? What kind of a world is this? With blood in my mouth and panties ripped, I staggered up the stairs and down the street wondering what to do. Almost in shock and very weak, I managed to stop a patrol car with two officers inside. "I was just attacked. What can I do?" "Well, there is nothing you can do unless you have witnesses, people who saw it happen." That surely didn't make sense to me. I just could not imagine people standing around, watching for crimes to happen, so that they could testify on court. The policemen did not even offer to drive me home or to a doctor, just drove off and left me standing there with blood running down my face and a terrible pain in my ribs.

Stanley was amazed and upset to hear how helpful the police had been. When I showed him the ugly bruised spot where my ribs were hurting so badly, he took me to see a doctor immediately. The x-rays showed nothing really serious, only a couple of bruised ribs. Taping them, the doctors ordered me not to return to work; I definitely needed a few weeks rest.

So Stanley went out and amazed me by getting a job as a delivery man for a commercial photographer.

I could well understand why Stanley was so reluctant to work, at least one of the reasons. His new boss insisted that either the beard had to go, or Stanley had to go. For once, he decided to give in – the beard had to go. He took his razor into the bathroom and locked the door. When he walked out again, my mouth sagged open. Here I was looking at this young face, this really young face! With his beard, Stanley had looked about thirty. What a shock to see him looking so young! Stanley had a slim jawline and high cheekbones, and a dimple in his chin, and I never realized how sensuous his mouth was, how pretty he was.

One of Stanley's problems, it seemed to me, was irresponsibility. His mother had never let him be independent. Stanley was her favorite child and during the time that he was in college, she would send him money, which he would spend on a motorcycle, for instance. Being the way she was, Clara would send him more. Stanley had never stood up on his own two feet, and when I met him this was what I had to face. But I loved him so very much, and I could see a beautiful person in him if he would just learn this one lesson, this one problem that he had never mastered.

Another idea that was floating around, and had been floating around for quite some time, was for me to have a baby. Deep inside I felt the time had come. I thought it might help Stanley assume responsibility because he really didn't have to care for me, but a child being dependent upon him might change his attitude. So we sat down together and talked about it. He seemed very happy about the idea, and the decision was made.

Now that Stanley and I had been together for about two years, we decided to save our money for a vacation in Tennessee. I Stanley would be meeting my family for the first time.

I was really happy to see them again! My father David was a real family man, he and Peggy having to provide for five children. He sometimes worked two jobs to make ends meet! I found out that Peggy's new son was born in October the same year as Jo-Jo, which meant that he had an uncle one month younger than him! Everyone in Tennessee assumed JoJo was Mom's son. She had visited before and of course told them he was her baby.

Sheila was the first of Dad's children and the only child that Mom and he had. Over the years, he and Peggy had procreated five children: Johnny Allen was their first-born and a beautiful blonde blue-eyed boy, quite spoiled because he was the first. Debra Jean was next. She was also blonde and had hazel eyes. Then there was Michael Wayne. He was real cute with a little darker complexion and dark golden hair. He looked like Daddy. I called him my little prince. Just before I left Tennessee at age fourteen, Glenda Sue was born. She looked like a porcelain doll with brown eyes and copper colored curls! She was the one I dressed up and carried around before I left. So now I had a new baby brother named Doyle Ray.

Dad's family was lively and they did not have much money but a lot of love. Stan loved them and they loved him. He was like a big gentle giant to them. Peggy and Dad gave us their own bedroom and slept on the couch, and we stayed for two weeks!

One day, we went to visit Grandma. She told Stan that I was the strangest child she had ever seen. She had raised seven of her own and two grandchildren. She told him that I asked such questions that she could not always answer them but had made her think. She also said I was satisfied with what I received and never complained like other children had. "She was like an old lady in a little body and somewhat of an angel, she obeyed so well!" she said. She said she was keeping my letters. They meant so much to her "Thank you, Grandma!" I laughed as I hugged her and told her I loved her. She loved Stan and called him her big teddy bear! It was really wonderful to see her.

Shortly after returning to Chicago we learned that I was pregnant! Stan was happy and thought it was ironic that I had conceived our first child in my father's bed! I guess it was symbolic!

Sometime later, we were in a restaurant in Old Town and had met an astrologer. The man was talking to us about astrology and Stanley was greatly interested in it at the time, and had three books on the subject. I was very quiet and just sitting there, with my eyes closed. I thought about the ship that Stanley and I had seen the other night so close that we had chased it with our motorcycle, hoping that we could see it, by the water tower ... I felt drawn, for some reason I had to find this ship, and I had seen it a couple of times.

All of a sudden I received an inner message from my uncle, and it said, "We've been trying to contact you. Your father Deashar has been physically very ill since he's been living in the physical world; he translated, and he was sorry for the way he had treated you; he realized it was selfish and that he was wrong in his attitudes, that he should have spoken to you and met you, and embraced you as his own child. Only his pride and his ego kept him from doing so. He tried to contact you so that he would see you before he died, but he failed. And he knew that it was his own Karma to suffer this way. Now that he finally wanted to see you, it was impossible to reach you because he had refused to see you so many times before. But he was sure that he would see you on another plane of existence and sends his love."

I started to cry and when Stanley asked: "Sheila, what's wrong?" I told him word-for-word what I had heard.

I had told Stan of my origin and true home right from the start. He was fascinated and did not doubt it for a minute. I felt relieved to be able to openly talk to someone. So I had been telling Stanley about my teachings, about the Laws of the Supreme Deity, and I had pointed out to Stanley some of our spiritual beliefs many times.

One of them which he particularly liked is a very simple analogy about life and reincarnation. Man's life starts in one point on a circle. He is helpless because he is a child, and in a child's body. On his trip around the circle, which represents life, he will grow and change as he has experiences and lose a lot of his prejudices and attitudes, and if he gets into different spiritual paths will grow till the time comes for death when he reaches again the same point where he had started at the end of the circle. Then he is once again physically helpless, and very much like a child, but if he reflects upon himself he will see that he is a completely different person in his attitudes and in his physical vehicle, that he is no longer the same person as he started out to be, because he had changed so drastically in his experiences of life. When he comes back in a physical body for yet another lifetime, he starts where he left off in that last life, that person, that personality, that attitude, and gets into an environment that believes the same way as he did in his last life.

I will never forget what happened a few weeks later. Stan was going out the door to watch TV at friends. We didn't have one. He was going to see the documentary on Dr. Martin Luther King. "Tomorrow they march into Alabama," he explained and I said without a moment's hesitation: "Oh no. He shouldn't, he will be killed there." – "What do you mean" he asked. I said: "I know the South and they aren't ready for this. He will be killed!" – "Oh Sheila, I don't think so!" he replied and left.

The next afternoon I had a doctor's appointment for a check-up. I was in his office all the time reading magazines. On my way home, I saw policemen blocking all the intersections and crowds everywhere. What was happening?

I got off the bus. We lived in a racially mixed poor area. I was walking toward my house when I was thrown to the ground by a policeman, just as a brick flew over my head and broke a store's front window.

"Sorry Ma'am" he apologized, "but I knew you didn't see that brick coming." – "Oh my God" I scrambled to my feet with his help. "What is wrong?" – "There are street battles everywhere because Dr. Martin Luther King was killed." –

"How?" I asked. "It seems a white man did it, but I do not know for sure." He walked me home to protect me. "You better remain indoors" he said at my doorstep. "Thank you!" I replied.

I walked in. The windows were broken and the doors open. Stan stood there with a pale face. "Oh my God." He grabbed me. "I was afraid you were hurt. I can't believe this is happening!" he said. "You were right with what you said yesterday!" he said quietly. "How could you know? he asked. My simple answer was "I just felt that it would happen."

It hurt me to see how the people were reacting to this terrible crime. They were only making it worse! Martin Luther King was trying to teach love and his death had unleashed violence. That is a crime! It seems that humans haven't learned to pull themselves out of tragedy with dignity and grace yet!

It seemed there were a lot of people hurt in Chicago and destruction was great in many of the large cities in America in predominantly black areas. The black people felt lost without their great leader. Instead of standing strong in his memory they sank in a desperation and many militant groups emerged taking them in a more violent direction, preying on their weakness and sorrow.

We had to move from Old Town because of urban renewal as it was called. So we were relocated to another place –rent paid! This was of course a blessing to us because we were poor by most economic standards. Although I never knew it I thought we were doing well. So we moved to the South Side of Chicago, close to the beach. I loved the area, but now I had to cross the whole city each time I had an appointment with the doctor.

We still had the motorcycle and would visit Stan's parents. His mother Clara was horrified because I was five months pregnant. She made Stan feel so guilty that he finally traded it for a black 1969 Volkswagen beetle. I loved it, it was a cute little car.

We had received so many gifts already from Stan's family. They were paying all the bills from the doctor and the hospital as well. Our baby would have all it needed. Mom had assured me I was going to have a girl and I believe she felt it. I was so happy that it did not make a difference and I did not seek to find out. During my pregnancy, Stan and I often would bring JoJo to our house for weekends. He was so cute at almost three and we would go to the beach and he loved Stan's pancakes. Stan would cut the pancakes into small squares to make it easy for him to eat. I loved to see how Stanley treated JoJo. I was sure he would be a wonderful father. After taking him home, Mom called and asked how to cut JoJo's pancakes as he insisted he wanted them in little squares like Stan cut them. We explained and had a good laugh!

Just before the baby came we went to a big celebration with Clara and I loved to dress up in a red velvet dress and white lace collar which she had given me as a gift. After we got home around eleven o'clock – I was getting ready for bed and was in the kitchen – my water broke. I called Stanley and he swung me off my feet, grabbed my already packed bag and we were off to the hospital. I was half excited and half afraid. Stan was nervous but trying to reassure me that all was going to be fine, but also cursing everyone for not moving out of his way. I laughed: "Stan, we are driving a Volkswagen. No one in America takes them seriously. They look like big toys." He laughed: "Yeah, you're right. Remember when I had trouble with the motor. I pulled over and opened the back to look and a man slowed down. I thought he would offer to help. Instead he rolled down the window of his car and yelled: 'What's wrong? Did the rubber band break?' Because Stan is so tall, he made the car even look smaller. We laughed at the memory.

Finally we arrived at the hospital and I was wheeled by wheel chair (they won't let you walk!) into the labor ward. Stan was with me holding my hand. The pains were very strong but again I wasn't dilating enough. So I received a shot to dilate me. But it wasn't as painful as during JoJo's birth. Then things started to happen very fast and before they cut the cord they laid my baby girl on my chest so I could see her! She looked sort of like a wet sticky puppy. When they brought her to me in my room and I couldn't believe she was mine. She had little blue slanted eyes and a head full of jet black hair about two inches long – a lot of hair for a new born. The nurses were crazy about her and had combed her hair up into a point. My eyes filled with tears. She was perfect. Stan was glowing with pride. We called her Tobea Lynn. She weighed eight pounds four ounces. "Thank you, God, for my tiny precious little angle!" I sighed as I dozed off to sleep.

At first, Tobi looked very oriental with her black hair and slanted eyes, unlike myself or Stan. People often asked "Whose baby is this?" I being very proud would answer much to their surprise "Why? She belongs to me!".

Later, when she began to eat with spoons or forks at about two years old, she would do something peculiar. She would turn the fork or spoon and eat with the part you hold. I asked her why she wanted to eat this way – she was two at the time. She explained that is how she remembers that she used to eat. "When?" I asked. "Before I was your little girl." "What did you look like?" I also asked. She looked at me and her grandmother. "Not like you and not like grandma." This sparked my curiosity, so I began to search through magazines and asked her to show me how she looked before. Finally in a National Geographic magazine she pointed to a Geisha and exclaimed: "That's how I looked!" Wow, I thought, this is interesting. "Do you miss those times and those clothes?" I asked. "Yes", she answered. Then I bought her Japanese robes, sandals and chop sticks. She loved them, until one day while playing with a friend she ran to me and announced: “I am ready to be your little girl now. I don't need these robes and things from before.”

Children as Soul have much past experiences that are overridden by the rigid learning process here, because many parents lack the knowledge how to help these Souls in their new life to keep the awareness of their previous existence within their consciousness. Therefore their education is only limited to their physical surroundings.

If you observe a child as an aware Soul from the time of their birth, it is a good beginning. Also be aware of the individual talents the child may have or the way they behave, such as eating habits, playing, choices of toys or what they enjoy doing. It may give you a few hints as to their previous incarnations.

Chapter 7 – Re-encountering my Spiritual Teachings

Shortly after Tobi was born, I went to visit my mother and we sat down with some wine talking about spiritual beliefs. She was into Rosicrucians and while I was listening to her, I received the inner message that I should talk about myself. "Mom, I've been wanting to tell you something for a long time, and I think the time has come. But I don't know how to explain this to you. You'll think I'm crazy," I said hesitantly. "Well, go ahead. Tell me what's on your mind," she answered, "I know that you are a smart young woman. You're not crazy." "Well, I'm not really your daughter. When she was seven years old, Sheila was in a bus accident on her way to Grandma. She died and I took her place."

I told her that I was from the planet Venus and that I had been sent here for a great mission and to work on our mutual Karma. I explained to her my relationship with Sheila in another lifetime. I did not go into any details on my life on Venus, just that I had grown to love her very much because I had lost my Venusian mother when I was born. I felt the need to talk to her now so that in the future when the truth was revealed, she would not be shocked or hurt by the fact that I hadn't told her. I said, "I've never got a chance to really talk to you and tell you these things, because our life has been so full of violence and so hectic and I didn't know how you would accept it. But now I've seen that you got into some sort of spiritual teaching, you might have a deeper understanding of what I am trying to say."

She said, "Yes, I know what you mean. I know what you're talking about, Sheila, because I noticed that there was a difference in you and Sheila. But at the same time I couldn't admit it to my consciousness because of the fact that I loved you so much and that Sheila was the only thing that I had. To tell myself that you were something that you weren't was very difficult for me, but now that we've got it out in the open, I'm very happy and I love you just as much anyway, and you're still just as much my daughter as she'll ever be."

We embraced and cried. After that my mother and I went out shopping as we always did and bought things that Stanley did not approve of because he was into health food, like chocolates, milk shakes and stuff. We came back home and ate, and I left as usual before Pedro would get back. So I went home very excited and told Stanley about what had happened. He was intrigued about this and very happy for me.

When I had met Stanley, he was an atheist like his mother. Clara was from Israel and rejected the Orthodox Jewish concept of a God that decided if you were not Jewish you were considered equal to cattle. This sent her into Atheism and on a quest to support equal racial rights in which she was very active. She was among the founders of the first Peace Museum in Chicago. We had many conversations about spiritual topics and she could better accept what I explained about God being the Energy Source of all creation.

When she died in 1997 Stanley was holding her hand. She was afraid that she would no longer exist after death. Stan promised her that life would go on afterwards. Immediately after she had taken her last breath and closed her eyes she appeared to him and whispered: "You were right Stan, I'm still here."

Stanley had tried several new ways, but for me they all lacked the truth of the teachings I had known on Venus. I got sort of tired of following him through his different interests like Buddhism, meditation, astrology, Edgar Cayce and some other esoteric teachings. I know that on Earth there have to be many different teachings because of the many levels of consciousness. Those Souls who are ready, but have not yet discovered the true teaching, eventually learn that the religions, occult paths, philosophies, yogas, and other spiritual paths are here as stepping stones that will eventually lead them to the true spiritual teaching.

After finding a book about Paul Twitchell, Stanley was once again convinced he had found my teachings, but when he told me about "Eckankar", I was not very interested, because he changed his spiritual preferences quite often. So I went to hear a lecture by Paul Twitchell, only because Stanley begged me to come. I had to take Tobi, who was just a toddler, and when she fell asleep I wrapped her in a blanket and put her under the table in the back of the room where the books were sold. She was just able to crawl and had the habit of untying people's shoes. I did not want her to disturb the audience when she woke up, so my attention was more on her than on the speaker in front. Not a word of what he said actually reached me.

When the lecture was over, Paul walked directly over to me, even though there were quite a few people who wanted to talk to him. He asked me if he could speak to me alone. Did he notice that I did not pay attention? I thought with a bit of a bad conscience.

We went to his hotel room for privacy. I didn't know what to think when he smiled and asked me to sit. "I know who you really are", he said, "your real name is Omnec Onec and you come from Venus." I was speechless with surprise. "I have been studying in a monastery in Tibet for 15 years, receiving my initiations and getting permission to establish these ancient teachings in America. In Tibet, Rebazar Tarzs was one of my Masters. One time, he took me on a Soul Journey to Retz and to Teutonia. He pointed to you, a small girl at that time, and told me to remember you, as we were going to meet in the future. You would be playing an important role in helping me to establish the teachings." He explained his work in the States, writing books, sending out discourses by mail for home study, giving lectures and founding places where people could gather to study and meditate together.

At first, I felt so ashamed for not listening to his lecture. But when he asked for my assistance in his work, I gladly promised to do whatever I could, having the baby to look after and working as a waitress. When I told Stanley, he was as excited about this as I was.

However, we discovered that we had to have several initiations by Paul in order to work for his organisation. He told us that this was necessary in the physical world as a spiritual preparation for doing spiritual work.

Paul Twitchell was the first modern-day Mahanta or Living Master in the Western world. It means he has received the rod of power passed from the Ascended Masters to the chosen person. These teachings were to be taught by a living teacher familiar to the time and conditions of the people being taught.

The Ancient Teachings are the original truths that are the basis for all creation. They are the teachings of all advanced beings, physical and otherwise. Originally the Venusians were chosen to be the protectors of the truth, as they remained in harmony without any separation of their basic spiritual concepts. They also brought the Ancient Teachings here when Earth was colonized by the first physical people.

Later, the teachings were hidden for protection from manipulation by the controlling forces that ruled Earth after the fall of Atlantis. This was before the birth of Christ. Later, Christ began to study in Tibet under the guidance of Fubbi Quantz, an Ascended Master who lived in a physical body at that time.

Paul Twitchell began to make these teachings publicly known in 1965 to rise the consciousness of people on Earth.

This has been the goal of all Masters while on Earth and of course the forefathers of Earth people. At first, we had small meetings at our apartment for studying and meditating the Ancient Teachings. More and more interested people joined our group and finally we opened a small store front. It served as a meeting place for those who were interested could receive information and read or buy books. I used it one day a week to teach dancing to those who wished to join the dance classes. We even choreographed and filmed a group dance, which was shown at seminars. Then Paul asked me to prepare a dance depicting the Journey of Soul for a major event. Which I did very much nervous about how it would be received by previously fundamental religious people! However, it was very successful.

Then Paul wanted us to be in charge of the Youth Group of Eckankar. We held workshops on acting, music, art and many other cultural topics that young people could participate in during the seminars. Very soon we were very well known in the Eckankar organization and we were travelling all the time. Paul and his wife Gail became good friends. They were very fond of Tobi, who spent more time in their room than in ours at the hotels.

When Paul told me he wanted me to publicly share the story about my origin I was very nervous. I should give my first lecture to about 300 people. You could hear a pen drop while I was speaking, the audience was really mesmerized by what I told them. After hours of the seminars I would sit in the hotel lobby and answer questions.

Paul asked me to write a book about my mission here on Earth and promised to publish it. At night, when everybody was sleeping, I would speak into a tape recorder. Later Rainer, a young man I had met in Eckankar, who volunteered to help me, would type it and ask questions later. He also organized an interview with a local radio station for me. The reporter was very open-minded, people phoned in and a crowd stood waiting outside to see me afterwards. And I received big sacks of mail. I had letters from all over the world, it was unbelievable. So we made cassettes of this interview and sold them through the mail for $5. This is how Wendelle Stevens, a retired air force colonel and well known UFO researcher heard about me.

Stanley's mother Clara also heard the interview in the radio. She belonged to the Mensa Club, which is a group of people with a very high IQ. She called me to tell that they were discussing the possibilities and the logic of what I had said. She was so proud that she told them that I was her daughter-in-law.

After the radio show I was asked to appear on a local talk show. The TV show was horrible. It was called the Dave Baum Show on Channel 32. He had a small skit, making fun of and belittling aliens. It was a short play some students or young actors did before the show. He was out to ridicule me. He was pacing back and forth, asking all kinds of questions. "Where is your birth certificate?" and things like that. Finally he said: "Do something to prove that you are from Venus."

Calmly I said: "I'm here to share information, I'm not an entertainer. This is a waste of time and energy that I have to defend myself like I'm in court. It is like you had never been to Africa and had an African here. Instead of asking interesting things about their culture, you do like they don't exist. I'd rather discontinue this interview, because I don't want to get into a conflict. It is beneath my dignity to be treated this way." Then I got up and walked off the show. He lost his job for treating me this way.

The producers were apologizing and all my friends congratulated me for my courage, but it was a shock for me. It was the first time that somebody tried to ridicule me, and I had to learn how to deal with that.

One day, Stanley decided to attend the Woodstock Festival, a small town not far from Chicago. I had been to many love-ins at various parks in Chicago, where all the hippies would bring musical instruments, blankets, food, wine and dress outrageously. Some of them painted peace signs on their faces and everyone wore flowers and beads. They would spend all day until late at night singing, playing music and making friends. It was always interesting with a real nice loving atmosphere.

Melitta our landlady lived downstairs and Stan and I in the upstairs apartment. Melitta loved Tobi as if she was her own child and she was glad to babysit, so that Stan and I could go to the festival.

Stanley told me that Woodstock would be the biggest love-in and the blast of the century because many famous bands and folk singers would perform. Well, it was not like all the be-ins and love-ins I had been to. There were about 20 acres of land with a stage and sound system set up. It was part of a farm and permission had been given by the owner. People came from all over America! There were thousands of wild people.

We had brought food and sleeping bags. You could barely find room to sit down and spread your blanket. There were portable toilets, thank god! The music was good, I remember that Jimi Hendrix played a song about Sheila. I knew it did not mean me, but it was interesting and I felt important to Stanley. I did not walk around like I usually did for fear of getting lost. People were drunk, high and whatever. Some were naked, running around with painted bodies and beads. Some had sex in the open! There was pure abandon of any kind of normal morals.

Anything goes seemed to be the motto, except for me and a few other not so freaked-out Souls. Stan wanted to stay the whole three days or so. He loved to get high. I told him that

I would only stay that day and night – so he could sober up and then I wanted to leave because it was too wild for me.

Even strange guys would ask me if I'd like to ball. "What was that?" I asked Stan. He told me that it was a hippie term for sex. My goodness, I thought, how can these strange men ask me such personal things in such a way! Stanley thought it was funny, but I did not! I did not sleep much because the party never ended. Music and everything continued all night, with people tripping in more ways than one. They stumbled over our blanket and sleeping bags, apologizing and saying peace and love. Always offering joints, wine and beer that was spilling as they danced and stumbled around. I do not know how Stan slept unless it was wine and pot.

When it became light, I was ready to leave. Some people were passed out in heaps it seemed to me. Stan agreed and it took us two hours to find our motorcycle. Empty wine bottles and beer cans everywhere and people grabbing us to dance, hug or whatever. It was more than I was prepared for. I might look like a hippie but I could not really fit into such a way of living. However it was certainly unforgettable!

One day I recognized that I was pregnant again. I continued my work for Eckankar as long as possible; but I gave up my dancing performances as I was too pregnant to perform live. Instead, together with Stanley's brother Mark I created a film with various locations depicting spiritual dimensions. Mark created this film as a project for the Columbia College film-making school he attended. The film was then used at all Eckankar seminars.

Even though I was pregnant we moved to Indiana, because Stan had found a job there. As I was to have the baby at home with a special clinic (Planned Parenthood), we arranged to have the baby at Blanche McLellan's apartment in Chicago. She was an Eckankar friend about 60 years old. So that is where we went about a week before the due date, however the baby had made other plans.

As the due date passed, I became bigger and bigger in the stomach, I had to be helped to my feet. The rest of me was the same, I looked like a potato with toothpick arms and legs. The doctors assumed I had the wrong date of conception, but I knew the baby was late. I was right, and after taking castor oil which I was told could induce labor I went into labor. The medical team came and spent their whole shift with me while preparing everything they needed. They covered everything with newspaper which they explained was sterile because of the ink! Ink was known to be a natural disinfectant.

Just before birth, they discovered that this was an unusually big child and moved me from the bed to the kitchen table. I was having natural birth without drugs. Blanche and Stanley were to assist by holding my legs, until Stan began to feel sick and was dismissed to get air.

It was a boy, and he weighed more than 12 pounds! They discovered that he was three weeks late, because the afterbirth was dried out. If he had not come now, he would not have had any food. We had decided to name him Zandar Onath, an ancient Venusian name meaning "accomplishment" or "prophecy fulfilled".

Zandar was looking like a 3-month old baby. I discovered that the new-born diapers were too small as well as the infant clothes I had bought for him. So we pinned a kitchen towel on him and wrapped him in a blanket before we placed him in a plastic laundry basket. I was crying because I had no fitting clothes for my poor big baby. So we pinned a kitchen towel on him and wrapped him in a blanket.

The head of the Planned Parenthood Organization was a 90-year-old woman. She climbed three flights of stairs to see the biggest baby they ever delivered at a home delivery. So she was impressed with Zandar, but a bit dismayed at his lack of clothes and diapers. She left reassuring me that she would make sure he received clothes and diapers or pampers which were now new on the market. I was very happy! So was Zandar – even if he couldn't express it yet!

Paul Twitchell saw Zandar for the first time, when he was about three months old. Paul knelt down in front of the baby who was in a little automatic swing and gazed into his eyes as he was welcoming this Soul to Earth. When he was ready to leave, he told me to take very special care of Zandar as he is very special for the future of Earth and more precious than gold!

After the birth of Zandar, I was pretty weak. To recuperate, the time I was allowed to spend in Ithaka, New York, at a big farm, helped me a lot. This farm belonged to Anja and Frederick Fuss, very good friends of Paul Twitchell. Paul gave strict directions to Anja "Feed her lots of steak and liver and spinache, build her back up, help her with the baby and help her work on the book". Anja and Frederick, who was a linguist teaching at a college in Ithaka, went through the manuscript together with me and we developed it.

We were living a harmonious community life and many Eckists went in and out. It was a little hippie-like, we grew our vegetables, produced our own yoghurt and often we danced and sang. Sometimes, we organized seminars here.

In 1971, Paul Twitchell suddenly died. I was inconsolable, because I had no opportunity anymore to speak out with him, because unfortunately there had been a misunderstanding between us over an interview that had appeared in a newspaper about me, making me look very arrogant and selfish. I did not know about this article, never had given the interview in the way it was printed and demanded a correction in writing. The lady reporter agreed to send a letter to Paul who was very upset about this. I was looking forward to meeting him at a seminar in Ohio. But Paul had suddenly died, shortly before I arrived. I was devastated that I did not have a chance to see him a last time and clear this thing up between us. I was told that he had left a cassette tape with a message for me, but I never received it.

Instead, Paul appeared to me in my hotel room that day and assured me of his support. He told me to adhere to my message, not let myself be influenced by other people and keep the teachings pure. He already foresaw the difficulties in the organization because it now was part of the physical and therefore subject to its rules. He assured me that he would continue to support me from the higher realms. I had to think of this conversation over and over again, because with Paul's successor Darwin I did not get along well. I felt that he didn't live up to his mission as the Mahanta. He did not approve of all my participation and slowly I became less active in the organization. After sending him my manuscript to be published, he notified me that it would not be published through Eckankar. It seemed that fate had a different path in store for me.

Having met Paul had really changed my life on Earth for good, but apparently it was not yet the right time to make my mission known all over the world.

A few years later, I met Harold Klemp, who became the new Mahanta, Living ECK Master in the year 1981. I got to know him as a gentle, humble man. Since then, he is giving the teachings of Eckankar to the people in a modern way keeping with current developments.

Stan and I were living in Chicago again and enjoyed living as a family very much. I was pregnant again with twin boys, when one night Pedro came looking for JoJo. My mother and he had separated and she was living in Texas at that time, working and taking care of JoJo. But as he was not allowed to enter school in Texas at the age of 5 but could do so in Chicago, she had sent him to me. I agreed let Pedro come and visit him. But after the first time, JoJo was so upset and crying that I asked him not to come again. I did not trust him and feared that he might try to kidnap the child. So my mother came to take him back to Texas.

The night she left, there was a knock on the door at three in the morning. When I asked who it was, I heard a young Spanish voice. Assuming that there was some emergency with our Puerto Rican neighbors, I opened the door on the chain, but it was Pedro and one of his sons from Mexico. He kicked it open, rushed in and grabbed me by the hair, threw me against the wall holding a straight razor at my throat. He would not believe me that JoJo was no longer there. In Spanish, he ordered his son to kill me. When I tried to run from him he knocked me down and violently kicked me in the stomach.

I screamed for Stanley who came running from the bedroom, struggling with his robe because he always slept naked. Pedro jumped on him and they fell to the floor. I managed to get to the door to scream for help. By the time the neighbors came out, Stanley had managed to throw Pedro down the stairs, he being a big man and Pedro a small one. He and his son ran out of the house, the sons of our neighbors followed but could not find them in the dark.

Stanley had cuts on his arms from the razor and I was a nervous wreck, when I noticed that I had blood all over me. But it was not from a cut, I was losing my babies! I was rushed to the hospital and lost one of them. It came out in pieces, from the brutal way he had kicked me. The doctors did not know what injuries the other might have and if it could be saved. I told them that I did not want a baby that might be damaged and decided to have an abortion. It was dangerous because I was five months into the pregnancy.

I knew that abortion is not a sin. You cannot kill a Soul. And of course you can reject it, if there is a danger for you or the child through illness or whatever. You have to make the decision if you want to have this responsibility, if you are ready for it now. There is a connection to this Soul and it will be returned to you somehow. Even if you cannot have children of your own, this Soul will come to you by family or friends and you will have a special connection to it. Then you will be able to give it the attention and love that it needs.

In the following weeks, I was terrified. I never slept. Every night I was afraid that Pedro would come back, with every sound that I heard I thought it was him. We had reported the attack to the police. But they never found him, but arrested a man with the same name instead. The poor guy was locked up in a prison cell for a night, until the misunderstanding was cleared up in the morning – much to the man's family's relief. Even though the police had assured me, they would not arrest anyone until I identified them first.

And on top of all this, there was another terrible incident. Somebody put a bomb in the liquor store next door. I had just turned away from the kitchen sink, getting a drink of water in the middle of the night, when I heard a big explosion. All the windows were blown out and our big oak kitchen table flew across the room. It would have killed me if I had still been standing at the sink. The whole place was full of glass, my ears were ringing from the sound and I was in a panic. I did not know whether it was gas from our stove or what had happened. Stanley grabbed Tobi and Zandar and we ran outside, barefoot and in our nightgowns. I was in a shock for days.

Then I fell very ill. I was passing out with my monthly period and was throwing up and having diarrhea all the time. At first, they thought it was appendicitis, but I had developed a tumor in one of my ovaries. After the abortion, some tissue of the pregnancy had been left inside me, and that was now poisoning my body. I was in surgery for eight hours to remove the tumor and the ovary. They also had to remove the appendix. I was in surgery three hours longer than expected and had to stay in the hospital almost three weeks.

Meanwhile Tracey, my best girl friend who had two children was keeping Zandar and Tobi, bringing them to see me through the hospital window. As they had to stand down close to the parking lot and I would wave and throw kisses. They were too young to be allowed to visit me. As the hospital was within a few blocks of where she lived, she brought them daily so that two-year-old Zandar could see that I was still there. He was afraid. As to his feelings, I was gone forever, as to a child every second is a long time.

She agreed to let me stay with her for several weeks after I was released – because of strict orders from the doctors that I had to rest and could not do so with two children alone. Stan would come after work to see me and play with the children and help with putting them to bed by reading their favorite books.

I loved Tracey like a sister and we usually were together on a daily basis anyway. However, I started to feel bad, even though I was resting. My appetite was not good and I had trouble breathing.

One morning at about 2.00 a.m. I was feeling real weak and had gone to the toilet, when I started to feel as if I was losing consciousness and tried to call out for help. I was so weak that I could only manage to whisper as I was collapsing onto the floor. Suddenly there was Tobi, who was about 6 at that time, standing in the door: "Mommie what is wrong? I heard you yelling for help!" – "Please get Tracey, I am really sick", I whispered. Tracey ran next door to a young man who was working at the hospital. He carried me out to his jeep and rushed me to the hospital, where they discovered that I had pneumonia with complications due to surgery.

Thank God for my daughter's psychic connection! Even though I was too weak to call for help she heard me yelling in her sleep in a closed room four rooms away!

To make matters worse, I developed an allergic reaction to the medication they gave me to clear the lungs of fluid.

I asked the nurse to remove the needle from my arm. She replied that only a person who is specialized in the intervenious medications could remove them. I began to lose consciousness then. I heard the doctor yelling at her that when a patient says it is making her sick, you don't wait until darkness closed in.

I was so weak and ill that the doctors called my family, afraid that I would die. When I slowly regained consciousness I saw – almost like through a fog that was beginning to clear – Clara, Hans, Stanley, my mother standing around my bed crying. When finally I was able to speak they were all trying to hug me. When after three more weeks at the hospital I was released, I weighed only about 90 lbs. All this was very traumatic for me and it took me years to get over these experiences.

Image 10: Omnec with Paul Twitchell wo brought the Eckankar teachings to the public. Omnec is pregnant with Zandar.

Image 11: Omnec with daughter Tobi and Stan with son Zandar in front of a wallcover with the Masters Fubbi Quantz, Lai Tsi and Rami Nuri.

Chapter 8 – Children, our Future

As soon as my health had improved and I had finally gained some weight, Stanley and I started to have serious problems.

We still had a very good understanding and communication, shared a lot of common interests and had a lot of joy with the children. But he was an emotionally very weak person, probably due to his experiments with drugs. Even though he stopped taking any drugs when Tobi was born, I felt that the effects were still with him. And I just could not cope with his lethargic, depressive states. I was waitressing, taking the kids to babysitters, doing all the housework, and he would do just nothing, not even talk to us or respond in any way for days. I could not handle the situation anymore and did not feel this strong physical love for him anymore. Part of my leaving him was because he was not true to me. He had other women and that was very devastating for me. This had destroyed the trust between us and I felt that I could no longer rely on him.

I took Tobi and Zandar and went to Tennessee to live with my mother for a while. She had married a wonderful man, Jay Hobson from Texas. I loved him and so did my children. They accepted him as their new grandfather very naturally. Mom and Jay wanted to adopt JoJo, because JoJo was embarrassed to have a different last name.

He was about twelve when I told him that I loved him as much as any of my children and would not adopt him to Mom and Jay unless I was certain that he wanted it. He assured me that it would make him happy.

Jay was a very good father and he loved Mom, of course. So they were a lovely family, living in a beautiful three-bedroom Ranch-style brick house. It was located in a beautiful scenic area outside Chattanooga. I always felt that Jay was more like a father to me than any other man Mom had married after Sheila's father. So I was happily living with them together with Zandar and Tobi.

One evening they invited me for dinner and we went to one of the better restaurants in town. There we met Bud. My mother knew him from before when I was living at my Grandmother's as a child. He was much older than I and he used to play in a rock and roll band with my cousins and came to practice at Grandma's house.

He instantly fell in love with me and I fell in love with the security he offered. He was very conservative, had a good job and did not want his wife to work. I felt that he could give me and my children the kind of security that I never had before.

But in this relationship there were other difficulties. Having lost his wife when their daughter Sharon was only 18 months old, he lived together with his mother, raising the child in their strict protestant way. They forced the little girl to go to church all the time, which I thought horrible. Bud's mother rejected me totally, being from the North, wearing make-up and the way I dressed. Being flamboyant and too outgoing – everything about me was completely against what she believed in. I came into a very close-minded society, very reserved towards outsiders. And prejudiced!

She was very bitter against me because I took her son and her grandchild out of her home, just living together. We only got married two years later when I was pregnant with our son Jason. At first, she did not even talk to me in my own home and I felt so humiliated about her behavior. I was trying to be respectful and tried to overcome it somehow in a loving way. It took quite some time but gradually she accepted me.

Bud's father was paralyzed after a severe stroke, being in a hospital bed in a small room next to the living room. Whenever we came to visit I made all the children and Bud go in and talk to him, because I liked him very much and wanted all of us to be respectful to him, too. I think this also made her change her mind about me. And I bought her candy and other things she liked. It took a long time, but finally my way of treating her with respect and love turned her around.

We lived in an old farmhouse at the foot of a hill with a little creek passing by in front of our doorsteps. We had to cross a small bridge to get to our farm. And fortunately the children's school was only five minutes away. We had put a lot of time and effort into renovating the house even though we had no central heating and I had to cook our meals on a huge wood-burning stove. I loved living in the country and being with the kids all the time. They enjoyed it as much as I and we spent almost all day outside.

I never had this before, because I had always been working ever since I was fourteen years old. Bud was working at night, so I also did my housework at night to be free for the children during the day.

We had a pet raccoon. I got it from the lady of a zoo which was overpopulated with raccoons, she said. They could not be let out into the wild, because they had reversed their natural instincts of sleeping, and would not be able to survive in the wild when sleeping at night and being awake during the day. So we took one and named him Rocky, after a Beatles song. We loved him very much, took him for walks on a dog leash. We learned quickly that we were not to get close to a tree, because once he got hold of the tree, we had to pry his little hands off. They really have a grip!

He lived in a little cage, but he would cry so that we let him out to play with the kids, chasing him around. They would hide behind the curtains and seeing their feet stuck out he would jump on them. And he would open the drawers in the kitchen, going from one to another. He was so fast, we could not catch him. He would climb up the curtains.

Once we went on a trip, leaving him in the bathroom, believing he would be ok in the small room with the water. He liked water very much. Returning home, we saw what chaos he had made: he unrolled all the toilet paper, turned the water on in the sink and in the bathtub, had opened the medicine cabinet, squeezed out all the tooth-paste, threw the brushes all over the room. He opened all the medicine bottles and dumped everything out, but luckily did not eat any pills. It was disaster. But it was real nice that he went to the toilet in the bathtub. It took me hours to clean up the mess.

During this time, I had no opportunity to attend seminars or give lectures, because of the ultra-conservative attitude of my husband and the way we were living. Maybe it was also to protect me from negative forces that were against my mission. Obviously, the time was not right to be active any other way, so the Masters had decided to give me the mission of working with children in the dream state, and some adults as well. There was a family in Arizona who told me later that I was actually appearing to them in the room. It was amazing. To this day I actually meet children who remember me from that time.

I was teaching them on the Astral Plane, playing, drawing pictures, visiting the temples and talking to the Masters about the other dimensions. We shared spiritual insights, did mantras and meditation, dancing. There was a lot of joy in it. I did not do it consciously all the time, but sometimes I was aware of it. Going to the Astral for study or talking to my people was something I had done all my life.

Some of the children I met had just died, mostly a violent death being mistreated or neglected. It was my task to help healing them and finding new parents for them when they were ready. Suddenly I discovered that I was pregnant with another baby. What a shock! I had had my tubes tied and only one ovary. It was certainly a miracle to become pregnant and it was destiny again.

My mother and Jay were very happy. They loved to have all the children on the weekends. We spent a lot of holidays with Mom or Bud's family. My father and Peggy in Chattanooga often came to visit along with my sisters and brothers and their children. It was good to share time with my Earth parents.

When Jason was born he weighed 8 lbs. 6 oz and at first he looked like a little red bull dog. Later he turned into a cute little blonde blue-eyed angel. All the children adored him, to say nothing of the grandparents.

It certainly secured my place with Bud's family. When the baby was two months old, I took him to visit Bud's father. He was thrilled to have a grandson by his only son. He held the baby in his good non-paralyzed arm. "Boy, he is a big one!" he said." Bud's father died one night later! I felt that he had been waiting to see his new grandson before he left.

Some difficulties arose because of Bud's prejudiced attitudes towards other races. He was also used to getting his way as he was spoiled by his family, being the only son. When Bud would rave about blacks, Arabians or whatever, even turning off the TV if we were watching a show about a black family, Jason would scoot real close to me and whisper. "We like black people, don't we, Mom?" I would say yes and don't ever forget it! I told the children that they could not argue with him or disrespect him, but to accept the way he was and to remember what I had taught them.

Growing up in the south, I was constantly confronted with racism. In the Government housing project where we lived, no black people were allowed at that time. It was only for poor white people. The black people had their own section of town called Nigger Town.

God having created all races, it is not right for human beings to judge what races they love and what they consider inferior. This is an attitude I cannot understand. It makes human beings superior to God, judging his creation.

When I lived with Bud in the 80ies, I remember a terrible incident that happened in Falling Water, the community we lived in. There was one entrance to the town. You had to cross a little bridge from the main highway. Every year on Halloween, the hoodlums would pile car tires on the bridge and burn them. So nobody could get in or out until the fire was finished. The year before, a man had died of a heart attack because the ambulance could not get to him in time.

So, this year, there was a TV team from Chattanooga to film the event. Part of the news team was a black man from New York. When he climbed out of the truck, the hoodlums took him and tied him up, telling him they were going to hang him. The man was scared to death and the guys just thought it was funny. When the police came to free him, he was in shock and insisted on going back to New York immediately. He never finished the news coverage and quit his job.

I knew the leader of the gang. He was the father of one of Tobi's classmates. I told my kids that this is a horrible thing to do and that he would suffer for what he was doing. Only two weeks later, he died. He was electrocuted while repairing some wires on a telephone pole. He slipped and fell into some water at the foot of the pole and touching the wires he was killed. At first I could not believe it when I heard the story.

For a while, I had my 83-year-old great uncle with me after my grandmother's sister had a stroke. I moved him in with us as he was active and I did not want him to be put in a home. When my great aunt fell into a coma because of kidney failure, we were summed to the hospital: my mother,

her brothers and sisters, my family and Poppy, my great uncle. The doctors said that they could keep her alive on machines. I felt sorry for Poppy as he stood there crying and holding her hand. They had been married about 50 years. She was the only member of my grandmother's family still alive. Now Poppy had to make a decision. I held her other hand and told him: "You know she is dying and it won't be good to keep her in suffering on machines." He nodded his head. I then talked to her. "Aunt Dellie", I said, "I know that you are afraid and that you can hear us. If you are reluctant to leave because of what will happen to Poppy, please know that he can stay with us and will be fine. We love you and wish you could stay, but not like you are. So if you have to go please know that Poppy will join you when his time comes."

Poppy wiped off his tears, bent over and kissed her saying "I love you, Honey!", then told the doctors not to put her on the machines and let nature take its course. She died that night. So Poppy became part of our family for three years before he left to be with Aunt Dellie. He was a valuable member, for the children really loved him and through him learned how to communicate and appreciate old people.

When Bud lost his job at the factory, he changed. He blamed me for everything, became very possessive and jealous and violent towards me. He was very ill, having asthma and emphysema, but he stopped taking his medication. He was very headstrong about it. His whole personality changed. I knew that this was perhaps due to his illness, because the oxygen flow to the brain was also affected by it. He became aggressive towards the children and we had many arguments about it. He did not take very good care of himself physically, so he looked much older than he actually was. I did not find him sexually attractive any more and made all kinds of excuses to avoid sleeping with him. He became very conscious of our age difference and very jealous. Even though we were living 30 miles from nowhere in the middle of nowhere, I was not even allowed to visit my mother unless he was there as well. I could not wash the laundry at her place. She had a washing machine and we did not. I had to wash all our clothes in the bathtub instead with my hands. We lived in a 100-year-old farm house and had to heat the water on a big iron stove fired with wood. I still have some burn marks on my arms from accidentally touching the hot metal.

When Mom became ill and acted strange because of her manic depressiveness, he did not want to have her in the house and we had a big fight about that. We had a family reunion once, but as Bud did not want to go, I had to stay home with him. This became really unbearable for me.

When Jason was at the age of five, I left Bud and took my children with me. But my guilt feelings for having taken his only son from him brought me back again. Meanwhile, his health was getting better, he agreed to take his medicine and better cared for himself. He became self-dependent and repaired cars and small motors. But our relationship would not get better.

Finally, I decided to have a divorce, but to leave Jason with his father. It broke my heart to leave my child but on the other hand I knew that the separation from his son would have devastated Bud.

Again, this was a karmic situation of course. In another life, I had been Bud's wife and had run off with his son. I was pregnant and he never found us. So now in this life-time I gave him a son. Jason is his only son to carry on his father's name, as in the other life. His father being an only son, the family name would have ended with him. The family line was carried on through Jason, and that was important to them. I also knew that this wasn't a permanent relationship as Bud had no way of accepting my true heritage. When I had told him about myself he just listened and never mentioned it again.

Tobi and Zandar were already at Stan's in Chicago. They had been flown there by Clara. Now I needed some money for a bus ticket into the north for myself. Our school helped me. He loved all my children as they were intelligent and won many awards for poems and stories. Now he bought a lot of children's books and other books from me. I let Jason choose the books he wanted to keep. At bedtime, I used to sing one song each that the children chose and I made a cassette of these songs to leave with him. I also hung a crystal in his bedroom window and told him to think of me as it glimmered. It was hard to leave him at the young age of five. I knew he would be okay as I had spent a lot of time explaining he could come to visit in summer and that we would call and write. We made a vow to say good night to each other at 9.00 p.m. every night.

It was unspeakably hard for me to leave him, but although he was only seven years old, he seemed to understand my motives. I made an agreement out of court to split

custody between Bud and myself. Jason was to spend his summer holidays with me and live with Bud the rest of the year.

In Chicago, I had my own apartment in a nice neighborhood close to where Zandar and Tobi lived with Stan. They were registered with a good school right across the street. I had a battle with the principal of this school. Being also the superintendent of the school district, she had in mind to bus in underprivileged children. This meant bringing students from poor areas with much crime into safer schools with good quality. This was fine – however, Tobi was chosen as one to be transferred to one of the schools in the bad areas where there was much street gang activities. She was an honor student with awards. Stanley and I did everything short of getting arrested to fight for Tobi to remain in Lincoln Park School.

After one week of going to a school in one of the Gang areas, Tobi was terrified and did not want to return. At age 16, she decided to quit, work part-time and get her G.E.D. at home.

Then I got a job in the famous "Faces" night club. It was an elite club for members only or celebrities. I worked in the coat room at a higher salary plus tips. Sometimes there were two to three hundred dollars in tips alone! They offered Tobi a part-time job so she was working with me on weekends. We were thrilled because we had to dress elegantly at work. No jeans or sports shoes allowed even for the workers. We loved working at the club!

There was a big tunnel of light at the entrance, and the doorman would telephone the DJ. He would then announce every couple that came in. They also had movie production parties there and we met all the movie stars. Frank Sinatra, Bill Cosby, George Hamilton, Joan Collins, Chuck Norris and many others.

One night, I had dinner with Omar Sharif. He came into the club and started talking to me. "You seem to be an interesting person, you are so dignified and ladylike. It is so unusual meeting someone like you working in a place like this. Most women are here to get noticed and get into the movies." He told me that he was a gourmet cook and asked me if I would like him to cook dinner for me. Of course I was thrilled.

He picked me up at home and took me to his beautiful penthouse apartment overlooking the lake. He cooked an excellent dinner for me and we sat in front of the fireplace, sipping wine and talking philosophy. He was very impressed by what I told him about myself, coming from Venus and writing a book about my mission. He was such a nice person and a real gentleman. He kissed me on the cheek when we parted and I thanked him for the pleasant evening.

And I met Muhammad Ali, the boxer. That was a nightmare! It was a question of insurance and security that we were instructed not to take fur coats. People had to leave them in their cars or take them with them to their chairs. So there comes this huge big man and wants me to take his full-length fur coat. I had no clue who he was. I said: "I'm sorry, Sir, I can't take your fur coat." With his deep voice he replied: "Yes, you can." – "No, Sir, I'm instructed not to take fur coats." – "Yes, you can", pushing his coat at me and I kept pushing it back. Then my boss comes running in the side door, ordering me to take the coat. "Why?" I asked him, "you explicitly told me not to take any fur coats." – "You take it. This is Muhammad Ali! Don't you know him? He's world-famous!" – "Oh, I said, I'm sorry but I never heard of him!" So I took his fur coat and hung it up.

My colleagues made jokes of it for weeks. Little Sheila fighting big Muhammad. The next day when I came in, the DJ announced: "Here she is, Mrs. Muhammad Ali herself!"

My first Christmas in Chicago was very lonely. Tobi and Zandar went to Michigan with Clara and Stanley. JoJo was in Tennessee with Mom and Jason was with Bud. I had to work a party at the club on Christmas Eve. I was free on Christmas Day. Here I was, all by myself in my new apartment, remembering our last Christmas in Tennessee. The children had planned a Christmas play for me and Bud. They created a cute touching play with costumes and songs, complete with programs. Jason refused to play baby Jesus so they had to use a doll. He became a shepherd boy instead. Well, this was a different Christmas without the children.

How much fuller life is with children! I believe that children are a special gift sent to us and we have to care that they have what they need on all levels to survive here and to learn what they need to learn. I learned a great deal from my children. One of the greatest lessons was patience. The greatest reward was their love and to watch them grow into beautiful human beings that are a wonderful contribution to humankind on Earth.

I take it as a very special duty and honor to care for these special Souls entrusted in our care.

When children are born into the physical world they as Soul still have strong connections and clear memories of where they were before and what their existence was in their previous incarnation. We must remember as parents that this Soul could be older than our own Souls. We only provide a physical body for them and we have a connection from previous lives together. They choose to come into your particular family because of a bond with you along with karmic connections. Also you will be able to provide them with the particular circumstances that are necessary for their individual experiences for learning.

We should welcome our babies in this world by saying to them: "I know you are an old Soul and one that I know. I am happy that you chose to be a part of my life here." They always understand us, even if they are too small to communicate right away.

I always spoke to my children like this way from birth. I could actually see the response in their expression! It always really was wonderful to experience how fast they began to communicate by trying to make sounds. I had always sung to my children while they were babies and talked to them even when they were only a few days old. Telling them that I would do my best to inform them about life here. They knew that I loved them unconditionally and respected them as individuals with great intelligence.

I always talked to them like I would to any other person. Every morning I said "Good morning" and asked them how they felt. If they cried, I would say: "Ok, you do not like this place so much. But you will get used to it. I will try my best to make you comfortable, because I love you."

I showed them many things and explained them. The more you speak to the baby, the faster they learn, they feel more comfortable and are not so helpless like at the beginning of this life. They feel that we understand them and that we will always be there for them.

Our children are not your possession, they are individuals.

As parent we are to provide them with proper values and knowledge about themselves and this world. They must know that we respect their feelings and choices in life and that we will always love them unconditionally and even when they disappoint us. It is important to express to them how we feel about their behavior and the importance of loving and accepting others as we wish to be accepted and treated ourselves.

If we feel the need to discipline our children, we should also explain the reason. My children told me that when I punished them it was easily accepted because I also explained the reason why to them. Mostly because I wanted them to be the best human beings they could. I also taught them that they must learn to be responsible for all they do and achieve in life. I told them I would always help them, not judge but understand. However they must be the ones who choose the solution to a problem, and I would support their choice 100%. I told them that there is no situation or anything they could do that would cause me not to love them, for my love for them is limitless and forever.

I spent a great deal of time teaching them the basics of language, how to count at least to 100 and to spell and write their names as well as to recite the alphabet, before they were three years old. We spent a great deal of time drawing pictures and coloring. I read to them nightly and sang for them at bed time. We danced, made up stories and songs. I believe that you must keep alive the creative and imaginative abilities of each child.

Also very important is to not only to teach them but to exemplify the law- and value systems we live in. They must be taught equality and to protect and be kind to those less fortunate than themselves. To be responsible for themselves and respectable to all people and other living entities.

As a parent, you must above all be honest about yourself and any mistakes in your past or present. When presenting the facts about life be realistic and honest. No matter what age they are you must be willing to talk honestly about sex and reproduction. Also the responsibility for having sex, health, birth control and responsibility of such acts. It must also be stressed that sex is a normal and healthy function of being human. Teach them to assume responsible for everything they do. Instead of judging them, help them find a solution to problems. Always tell them you love them, you can never express this too much. Allow them to express joy and anger, so as not to repress and create blockages or psychotic tendencies. However, discipline is a necessity and lack of it can create criminal tendencies in humans and a lack of respect for laws and elders.

Even though I informed them of the Supreme Being, all my children were given the free will to choose their own religion when they were old enough. While they were growing up I allowed them to go to and explore other religions with friends of different religious faiths, so they could experience the various organized religions. I did not judge or speak against any of these.

Having four children was a task. I could actually write a whole book about my many humorous and surprising experiences with them.

When JoJo was three years old, he started to speak about a friend he called Statie. Everywhere we went he wanted to know if Statie could come also. He always played with Statie and talked to him. This continued until he was in school. I believe that his friends in school convinced him that it was his imagination and he started to doubt and lost his ability to communicate and see his friend. But he still remembers Statie to this day.

When I used to have meditation groups at home twice a week in the evening with several people we knew, the children would attend of course. They wanted to do the mantras as well and along with all their favorite stuffed animals, toys or dolls. Afterwards some would share their experiences that occurred in their meditation. Sometimes the children would draw the things they had seen or

heard.

Once, when Tobi was about 4, she exclaimed that she had heard snow falling. Some people explained that snow did not make a sound. I said: "Well, how do we know? Have any of you ever tried it?" I was interested in what it sounded like and convinced it was possible.

Of course, living in Chicago we had plenty of snow, but it was far too noisy. However, years later when Tobi was about ten and we were living in Tennessee in the old farm house, where it very seldom snowed, being in the South. One night in an unusually cold December, I had gotten up to check the fire in our wood-burning stove, then I saw that it had been snowing. It was around 1.30 a.m. The snow was about six inches deep. I went in and woke up Tobi. She was a little startled as I told her to come with me. As we tiptoed quietly through the house to the front door, I explained that this was our chance to hear snow falling. "You really remember that!" she exclaimed with much surprise. I told her, yes, I always wanted to hear it since her meditation experience. So laughing at the absurdity of going outside in our nightgowns at 1.30 am, we went out into the dark quiet night with the moon making the snow sparkle and it was still snowing. We sat on the ground and leaned our heads as close to the ground as we could. So one of our ears was close to the snow-covered ground. we held our breath as we listened and we heard it: tiny crystal-like sounds, almost inaudible, a precious tinkling sound as the falling snow flakes fell on the snow crystals already on the ground. Wow, be both exclaimed, you really can hear snow falling. We hugged each other as we laughed about the experience and then hurried in to get warm and dry.

When Zandar was only two years old, he always loved to play with the pots and pans which made it difficult for me to cook. So I asked Stan, Tobi and JoJo who was visiting to play with Zandar so that I could prepare dinner. They asked him what he would like to play with and he wanted the small wooden Charley Brown figures. Zandar chose Snoopy, Tobi wanted Linus, JoJo had Charley Brown. That left Peppermint Patty for Stan. I thought this was funny. When Stanley asked Zandar: "What are we going to do now?" he replied, "We are going to visit God!" We all thought this was funny but did not want to upset the baby. So we asked, "Where does God live?" – "On top of the refrigerator!"

Oh no, I thought, they are all coming into the kitchen. And here they are, on hands and knees, pecking along with the small wooden people pretending to walk. All of them arrived in the kitchen. Stan stood up and pecked his way to the top of the refrigerator. He was the only one tall enough to reach it. "Hello God", he said, "I'm Peppermint Patty!" Everyone laughed except Zandar. He stood there only in his diaper, pulling on Stanley's leg: "Don't be stupid, God knows who you are!" We all rolled on the floor with laughter. "I don't know whether to be insulted or impressed", Stanley said, "of course, you are right. You don't have to introduce yourself to God!" So far, we had never realized how much the babies understand.

At the time when Jason was four, he sat at the kitchen table coloring in a book. "You know, Mom," he said, "we are not really white. If I color the people white they look like ghosts. If I use peach, they look alright. So we are really peach!" A few minutes later he announced: "Mom, I know why God made black people! Because he ran out of peach paint and then used black!" I laughed, of course, because Jason had used all of his peach crayon and decided to have black people in his coloring book. And he assumed that this was what God did. Well, I thought, this is certainly an unprejudiced idea about races!

You must take time with children and play and laugh. Teach them to enjoy life and all it offers and to accept the difficulties as part of learning. Failing also is a part of learning how to correct our mistakes. We must be able to accept our negative aspects and our problems, as well to laugh at ourselves and to believe in the positive and goodness and support it with our energy. Never forgetting that our imagination is the key to all that is or will be.

Teach your children what you wished you had been taught, so that they don't have to search for the truth most of their lives. And they can spend more productive and creative lives toward a new world, for the children are the future.

Image 12: Omnec at the registry office with Bud, Tobi, JoJo, Sharon and Zandar.

Image 13: Omnec with her Earth father David and his first grandchild Christine.

Image 14: Omnec and her daughter Tobi in the Chicago nightclub Faces.

Chapter 9 – My Way to the Public

The following years of my life went by in a flash. After the Faces night club had been closed down I was back in waitressing. I worked at the famous restaurant "Zum Deutschen Eck", which is still included in each Chicago guidebook. The owner was a native Bavarian who had a traditional band in lederhosen performing every Saturday evening with the guests singing along. The female employees wore blue dirndl dresses with white ruffled blouse and apron. This is where I learned to like and appreciate the German cuisine. Years later, when I was visiting Germany for the first time, everybody was baffled because I could read the menu and ordered dishes such as pork knuckle with sauerkraut, even though I didn't speak the language.

I was enjoying my freedom and spent the weekends with good friends and my children. They grew up and became more and more independent, but we always kept our close contact. In turns the children were staying with me for a few weeks or months. I did not think about a new relationship, but fate brought a new man into my life: Emanuel. His younger brother, who was called Odie by everybody, was my next-door neighbor. We liked each other and became friends very quickly.

One day I rang his doorbell to return the iron I had borrowed. A handsome young man opened the door, who Odie introduced as his older brother, Emanuel. We liked each other right away and soon we spent all our spare time together.

His mother was of Irish descendent living in the South of the USA. His father was a prominent lawyer with forefathers from Puerto Rico and Africa.

Before we searched an apartment together, we had a long discussion about our age difference – I was 36, and then he was just 22 – and the problem of mixed marriages. Couples with different skin color have to suffer to this day under the prejudices of their fellow human beings and we were no exception. Once we had been almost arrested just because an overzealous police officer did not like to see Emanuel and me walking down the street together.

We lived together for about nine years and Emanuel became a permanent part of my family. One by one, Tobi, Joe, Zandar and my mother lived with us in our apartment. Of course, Jason came every summer. We had to bring Mom to Chicago when her manic depressive illness became a problem for her to live alone. Soon, we found an apartment around the corner for her and JoJo to share, within walking distance so that we could remain close.

At that time, I had a very good job at the apparel center, a fashion convention place in Chicago. I worked in the restaurant in the lobby of the building which catered to the convention people. I even got a position for JoJo to work with me. Meanwhile, Tobi was living in an apartment with a friend. Zandar had moved to California to attend college on a partial scholarship he had earned with awards and outstanding grades.

Tobi was attending one of the best beauty academies in Chicago. Jason was excelling in school and even working with me in the restaurant during the summer. All of a sudden Wendelle Stevens called me. I had communicated with him for years while living in Tennessee. Years ago, I had received a letter from him with a small biography telling me who he was. He had heard one of the many cassettes from the radio show in 1973. He told me that he was an ex-pilot on the Air Force and a retired Colonel now involved in UFO investigations. He was interested in my book. I had sent him a copy of the manuscript in 1980. He then was arrested and imprisoned for 5 years on false charges, so that he would not make publicly known what he had observed and the photos of UFOs he had taken would not be published. After his arrest, he wrote me saying that if I felt that a connection to him might be embarrassing, he would not blame me if I searched for another publisher for my book. I assured him that I was not concerned and wrote to him on a regular basis to his "federal hotel" as he called the prison.

When he was released we had a few phone calls to keep in touch. I had forgotten about the book off and on, as I was caught up in my mother's illness and working to survive. When he called to tell me that the book would be published and on the market in spring 1991, I was shocked. As I received the phone call in March, I was stunned. His plan was to present me and my book at one of the biggest ever planned UFO congresses in America. He was sending me money to have a special gown made for my appearance and my flight and stay were paid for.

I had to sit down to take it all in. This was it. It was now to be known who I was – not only to a few members of my family and my friends from Eckankar but exposed to the whole world. What effect is this going to have? I knew that it was an important part of my reason to be here on Earth.

Quite calmly, I remembered that I had prepared for this many lifetimes before. This was part of my real function here. That is what the Masters were preparing me for. I found myself a quiet spot and started to meditate. I thought back to my past connection with the Masters.

It began many lifetimes ago. After the Atlantean times, my first entrance into the physical was as a monk in Tibet, working with Fubbie Quantz, Rebazar Tarzs and Gopal Das. Rebazar and Fubbie were still physical at that time. Gopal Das was already an Ascended Master. They were my teachers in this life and my whole life was devoted to the teachings.

Later, I had a connection with St. Germain, when he was alive. I was one of his alchemy students. I was more interested in alchemy than spirituality in this life. I worked with him in his laboratory and was fascinated by the things he could manifest. St. Germain lived for a very long time, even centuries. There are many stories about him.

I lived a very special incarnation in the close environment of Jesus Christ. For this reason, it later became part of my mission here on Earth to tell unknown truths about this great Soul. I was shocked when they told me on Venus that because I had many connections to the Masters from many lifetimes and I am well set in the basic true teachings, I do not waver from that no matter what the influence is. The Masters told me that I had a choice: either take this mission or being born on Earth again because of the karmic ties that I still had here. But by being born on Earth, there will be many difficulties for me because of the divided brain and the strong influence it would be a struggle for me to remember the teachings.

It would be easier to do it this lifetime. I had to make a decision. There was a little anticipation and excitement about coming to Earth as I had been here before, but I was not familiar with the societies in the 20th century. The Masters gave me a little history but my problem was that I had difficulties with being interested in history. They gave me some scientific facts but it was the same thing: all this is too mental for me. I am more artistic and into expressing feelings and dancing and joy and fascination with things. So I did not put enough attention to the information.

It seems simple when you look at the many thousands of lifetimes that you have existed. Every lifetime looks like a grain of sand. It is so unimportant in your never ending existence as Soul. But when you enter into this little grain of sand then it really becomes so great and overwhelming. This is a shock for the Soul and that is why so many people get caught up in their difficulties and have trouble to remember that this is just another life, another grain of sand.

Shortly before I left Venus, the Masters called me: Rami Nuri, my Master on Venus, Fubbi Quantz and Rebazar Tarzs. They told me that they had special gifts for me. Remember, I was a little child and I was expecting something nice to take with me, a magic crystal or something nice to play with.

Fubbi said: "One of the gifts we are going to give to you, Omnec, is that on a very spiritual level you will be able to create a calmness in the people around you." Rami Nuri added: "We are giving you the ability to take something so complicated and difficult and make it so simple that the people can understand." Then Rebazar Tarzs said, "We will give you the ability and strength and patience that people can feel in this love to you, even if they disbelieve at first, the truth will connect to them and they will see very clearly."

And I am standing there disappointed, thinking these are not gifts, these are only words! And the Masters told me that these words will mean something to me later. It sounded very nice but to me it still was nothing but words and I was very disappointed to have no real presents.

They told me that I was going to have very difficult times, not always joy and adventure. "We know how you are and we have to see what the reception is. And as things develop you will be given more and more information and things to do. But only when we are sure that it is the right time. You must be strong through the difficult times. Please remember that we are not abandoning you even if it may seem that way and that your suffering is for a reason." It was the first time that I asked myself what I had done. This load is so heavy.

Later when I met Paul Twitchell, who was my Master here on Earth, he told me that he had seen me on Venus. This made me very happy because I have no proof. It is impossible to invite people to see the spaceships. It is for the protection of the Venusians, some of them have lost their lives through the attempts to get their technology. They do not fight back because this is against their spiritual belief. By many beings, the Venusians are considered wishy washy, because they will not destroy anything that is part of creation. They do not judge and do not criticize and so naturally they appear to others as being soft or weak. Through the last 40 years, I have been in contact with various Masters, meeting with them and sometimes not even understanding what they were telling me. Sometimes it would come in a dream, sometimes it was more real. I did not understand everything they wanted me to do, why I had to establish the Operation Peace program, for instance. I did it and only step by step, when they started to inform me about the Transformation Process I began to realize what was going on. Only when the Masters were sure that the Transformation was going to be successful, they told me to speak about it. Everything fell into place and I thought I now had the whole picture. But the Masters were shaking their heads telling me that my small picture is just a tiny piece of a bigger puzzle. They do not give me all the information because it would be overwhelming and would throw me into a panic of not being able to do this work as it is so much. And the future view depends on how many people are involved. We can only do it step by step, giving everyone his specific task. You are all working for the same cause and it comes together. But it takes a long time for you to see what you are doing.

In the future, there has to be a harmonic blending of the male and female energies. At first it was only female energy, then the male energy. We have a long lineage of male Masters, and there are only two female Masters and you might be the next one.

When they told me this, I stopped doing any kind of spiritual work for some time, because I did not want this responsibility and this position. "I do not think that I can do it. I want to be human. I want to be like everybody else and share the information but I don't want to be a guru or whatever." – "Well and that is why you must do it, because you don't want it," the Masters told me. "If you wanted it so much, it would be your ego taking over and then you would not be the right person."

Obviously, I have misused my powers in a past lifetime so that now I am always thrown into a fear of repeating this.

"You are a Master and people recognize it," the Masters explained. "They will patiently wait till they can look into your eyes. That is the Darshan. Their Soul knows that they have to receive this connection. Now it is up to you to let people know about their true heritage and that the truth has been hidden from them. That Soul has Its origin in another dimension. Remind them of their magnificence, their power and knowledge. Tell them about the transformation and show them how they can use their energy to support this process."

There are hundreds of Masters, Vonic, my teacher on Venus, was also one of them. To me, he was just a teacher, I did not have a clue of his true mission. All of the Ascended Masters are very old Souls who have experienced everything they could in the physical and then they make a decision that they will continue to give information either from the other levels because then they have the ability to manifest physically or not and to work on all levels. All Souls reach this point eventually. The Ascended Masters are nothing but people like us who have reached a certain level and made a decision about their future mission.

My Masters work with lots of humor; they are so tricky! When I am happy that I have some clearness they want me to be confused again. This is their way of helping me to handle it.

These are a few of the messages the Masters gave me. Even though it sounds quite confusing, if you re-read them there is a message. This is their way!

There is no copyright for the truth.

My only purpose in this life is to help you remember the things that you already know.

I can't remember what I have forgotten, but I must not forget what I already know.

People who think they are enlightened have lost their minds. Well, never mind, leave the mind behind and then you are enlightened.

After my long meditation and getting in touch with my Masters, I only knew that my life would change and I would be led in a natural way to do what had to be done. Of course I shared the good news about the release of my book and my appearance at a UFO convention with my family. They were all excited and happy for me. My friends' and fellow workers' reactions were from a mixture of disbelief, laughter and jokes to sheer fascination. My book and the idea that I was someone coming from another planet caused a great stir, and for weeks I was in the focus of attention. Several times people came to me during work, including the mayor of Chicago, and wanted me to sign my book. So I was sitting at his table answering his questions in my waitress clothes. My boss was very proud of having such a prominent employee, but to me all this hype was quite annoying.

Then the big moment finally came. I flew to Tucson, Arizona, where the UFO convention was to be. Wendelle had informed me that I was the surprise guest. No one was to know my true identity, as I was the last speaker. Many famous guests were there from many countries nationwide. One participant from Germany nevertheless knew me immediately, walked straight over to me and said, "Welcome to planet Earth".

For my protection, Wendelle kept me in a small motel about 3 miles from the big hotel where the convention was. I had body guards in a van with a two-way radio so Wendelle could inform them when I was ready to attend. I could sleep as long as I wished and call him any time in the afternoon when I was ready to come to the convention. It was wonderful. I just assumed that due to his experience with the CIA he was over-reacting. I did not feel any danger.

I had a very successful lecture, only interrupted by one man who wanted proof of what I said. He asked, "How do we know that you are 220 or even 41?" Another man replied: "I have met her 15 years ago and she does not look one year older!"

Then he began to argue about other dimensions. I quietly told him that he was wasting his time and mine. "I do not believe in debates as they are a waste of energy, and if you do not believe me it does not change what I am! Why are you here if you are not really interested?" Everybody applauded.

Wendelle came up and expressed to everyone how proud he was of me and what a wonderful lecture I had done at my first public appearance. I felt elegant in my new gown and was looking forward to autographing books. Wendelle rushed me, surrounded by his hired guards, out a side door. "Am I not supposed to autograph books?" I asked him. "Not yet! The trouble maker in the audience was a CIA agent and we have to clear the area and make sure it is safe for you in the lobby first." I could not believe it, it seemed like right out of a secret agent movie.

I was in for a shock: TV cameras everywhere, microphones shoved into my face from all directions, flashes from cameras. Then I was rushed from one room to another to be videotaped and interviewed by national and international press, TV and radio. One lady burst into tears as she was interviewing me for a UFO magazine. She did not know why but when she read my name she felt a sense of urgency and importance to meet me. I tried to console her by telling her that we had been very close friends in another life and she cried even more and excused herself.

Later she introduced herself as the president of the UFO library and an agent in Hollywood for prominent stars. She wanted to help me with my promotion.

Finally, I escaped into the bar to have a beer and signed books. Collee, the lady that had cried at the interview, and I became good friends and clowned around a lot in the following three days. With her video camera, she was pretending to make a commercial for beer. I was to take a sip and say "ahhh, that was worth coming to Earth for!" We were rudely interrupted by a young couple who told me that I was making a fool out of myself with these people who did not appreciate me. They tried to get me to leave with them, just short of force me, and became very aggressive when I refused. I was puzzled. Then Wendelle arrived to tell me that they were CIA people.

Back in Chicago, I had lots to share and everybody was calling me to say you are in this and that paper and I saw you in this TV station. I went back to work with a few changes. After work I would change clothes, run out to a limo and rush to a TV interview. I would announce that I would autograph books and give the address of the restaurant and actually giving autograph sessions in the bar. This was only the beginning. I had become the women from Venus. Most people who could not remember Omnec just called me Venus.

Image 15: Omnec with her four adult children: Front: Tobi and Omnec. Back: Jason, Zandar, and JoJo.

Image 16: Omnec with Donna and Jay.

Image 17: With Lt. Col Wendelle Stevens, who first published Omnec's autobiography "From Venus I Came" in 1991.

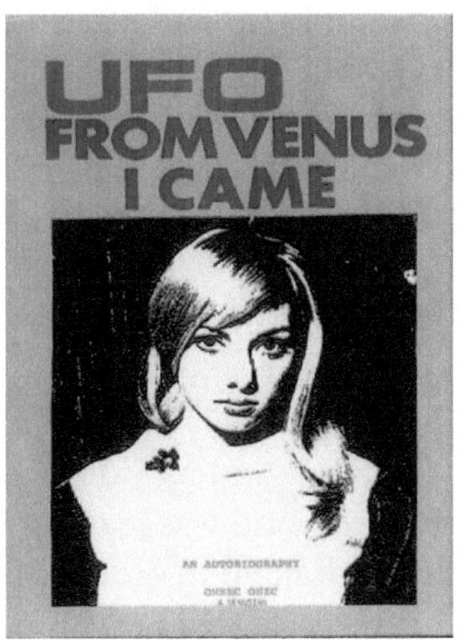

Image 18: "UFO From Venus I Came", original cover.

Chapter 10 – Fulfilling my Mission

As my life as Omnec burst into full bloom and I was flying to various states for conventions, TV interviews and workshops, my private life was in trouble. I had suspicions about Emanuel having affairs.

When I had conclusive evidence of Emanuel's betrayal with Gwenda, a young girl I had been helping through a traumatic experience that involved her father's sexual abuse, I decided that our relationship was over. I had treated her as my own daughter and she was sleeping with my boyfriend of many years. It was too much.

I took advantage of an invitation from Wendelle's grandson and flew to Arizona. His name was Gem and he was really nice. He offered to pay for my flight and I could stay with him at Wendelle's house. It seemed a good way to overcome my broken relationship. I also had offers for TV shows and conventions in California. These appearances were arranged by Wendelle and Collee. I had a wonderful time becoming acquainted with Wendelle's family and travelling. I also got to meet the family of Eckists who often had conscious contact with me on the Astral.

Gem and I spent a couple of days at a ski lodge. It was built by the Indians in their reservation in the White Mountains. Gem owned a cabin there, really high up in the mountains. Everybody was out skiing and as I do not ski I just sat in the lounge and had lunch and was reading a book. I had my book with me. When I wanted to order something to drink, this Indian came over and offered to share his pitcher of beer with me. He asked me why I wore white and I explained it to him, told him about myself and the spiritual work that I was doing. I showed him the book and told him a little bit about Venus. He asked me about my silver ring which a Hopi Indian had given to me many years ago and I told him the story.

Then he told me a little bit about his culture. He was hired to patrol all of the reservation at night and watch for signs. As an example he told me that if he saw an owl on someone's property, he would report this to the family, because this means that there is going to be a death in the immediate family. Also he was protecting the life-stock like lambs and such from wild beasts. He told me that he felt that maybe I was fulfilling part of their prophecy what they call the great white hope. After the birth of the white buffalo there was to be a white woman who would be a spokesperson for them and a spiritual enlightenment. All the Indians do believe that they were brought to Earth from elsewhere, so we talked a little bit about the races living on the other planets. After a while he said good-bye and left the restaurant shorty before Gem and his friends returned from skiing.

Several months later Gem called me in Chicago to tell me that he went back to the lodge for skiing with his friends. "You are not going to believe this," he said. "All the Indians are talking about you. They asked me where you are. They know all about you from the man who travels around the reservation and who had the conversation with you. You are a legend among the Indians!" Even though I was very fond of Wendelle and his family who treated me like a daughter, I returned to Chicago after a couple of weeks to take care of my family. Mom had been in and out of the hospital due to her manic depression. It was very difficult to regulate medication for her. A lithium over-dose would toxic effects and more manic attacks.

I continued to work at the apparel center and helped JoJo look after Mom. All of my children were very proud of my book and what they called fame. I did not feel famous. I felt no different from before.

I received an invitation to give a lecture in at a UFO convention in Düsseldorf, Germany, and have a dance workshop. I had not danced publicly for years and did not understand why they wanted a dance workshop at a UFO convention. I was excited about seeing another country. I had never been outside the United States except Mexico since my arrival on Earth. Unless a spaceship ride counts ...

Carmen, a lovely woman I had met via a radio interview and who had accompanied me on several trips to California and Colorado wanted to go with me.

So we prepared for the trip. I practiced a dance, chose some wonderful music inspired by my son Zandar and bought a leotard and dance shoes. I used the old dance costume from my years in Eckankar!

When we arrived at the convention hall, Marina Popovich ran over to hug me, leaving a lot of surprised-looking TV people behind who were just interviewing her. She was a famous Russian test pilot. We had met at an event in the United States and had become very good friends. Out of their curiosity of who I was she was greeting so warmly the TV people also wanted to interview me.

This was the first time that one of my lectures was translated into another language. It was kind of strange: when I just said a few words, the translator seemed to talk much longer. I managed to get through without too much panic. Peter, my translator later explained that translating from English to German would make a text about a quarter longer.

To close my lecture, I invited people of all ages to my dance workshop. I told them that to Soul age doesn't matter and hoped that considering the wide range of activities available at least a few people would show up at my workshop. I was presented a dozen red roses and Wendelle Stevens came up to exclaim to the audience how proud he was of me, because I had never spoken in a foreign country.

About 300 people had come to my first lecture in Germany. Many people applauded, but when I mentioned that I like beer and that I was going downtown to have one, they gave me a standing ovation. Fortunately no lecture was scheduled for me the next day. So we went to bed a little exhausted planning to get up at 8.00 a.m. the next morning because we wanted to see something of Düsseldorf. We got up with our travel alarm, got dressed and went downstairs. The room was empty and when we asked a lady for breakfast she stared at us like we were crazy, silently pointing at the clock. It was 2.30 in the afternoon. We had forgotten about the time change. We laughed our way out of the hotel and went to find coffee.

When going to bed the night before I had decided to have 30 people for my workshop even though only 8 people had registered by then. At the convention we were told that I not only had the most people in my workshop, but exactly 30!

To begin the workshop I did a Venusian-style dance and Carmen took photos. Renato, a man who became a good friend later, was making a video. Soon I had everyone dancing including the cameraman with the video camera and my interpreter Peter. He even offered to work for free if I ever returned to Germany. He had refused to translate for me at first because he did not believe my story. But he had really changed and when I asked the people what they had experienced in meditation he was the first one that wanted to share his experience.

Carmen and I planned to stay for a few days and wanted to know if there was anyone who could show us around. A handsome young man from my workshop volunteered as he had free days from his job at a Reiki center. We went to see the dome in Cologne and visited a nearby castle called Schloß Burg. There I had the eerie feeling that I had lived in this castle in another lifetime. On a mural in one of the rooms were paintings of members of the royal families that had occupied the castle. Among them, I found myself and Thorsten, the young man who was accompanying us.

A few weeks later, Thorsten called me in Chicago. He said he and the other workshop participants wanted to pay for my fare back to Germany to give another workshop in Eddigehausen. I thought it was wonderful to see him again and meet all these new friends. When I arrived there were far more than 30 people and the workshop was to take place in a very old huge house. This house was part of a castle that overlooked the house. It was owned by Eberhard von Hagen's family. This is how I met what I call my German family today. Ever since then the "family" has grown so much, I cannot mention all the names. However, I soon learned that it was part of my mission to meet these people.

In February 1994, my book was published by the Omega Verlag in German for the first time. We celebrated on New Years Eve with a nice dinner at Gisela's and Martin's – my first German publisher's – house and everybody who had worked on the book set out for the Rhine river to see the fireworks. When we were walking down the street, we saw a UFO – a big glowing orange ball floating silently across the sky. With the sound of fireworks nearby, we watched till it was out of sight. Poor Manfred worked all next day to determine if it was a hot air balloon or what else. Flying hot air balloons near fireworks is dangerous so we all settled on an UFO. We all held this occurrence for a good omen for the success of my book "From Venus I Came".

After the book was released, I gave interviews and was invited to many TV talk shows. I found out that Gisela had received so many calls and letters that she had the idea of sending me on a tour in Germany. This put me in a small panic at first but then I agreed even though I did not know what I would teach at the workshops. I knew I could do lectures and interviews. When I asked Uncle Odin and the Masters they simply replied: "You share with them your knowledge, perspective, and understanding." I knew then that I would have to learn as I went what I should do.

With my first tour in 1994, again a new chapter in my life had begun. I can only be thankful that whatever I needed came my way without asking and my life enfolded like a lotus, revealing more to me about spirituality than I knew.

On my numerous lectures and workshops I talked among others about the Spiritual Transformation of the Earth and its inhabitants, which is going to change life here into a paradise similar to the one that already exists on Venus. The transforming power of unconditional love plays a big role in this process.

While I was traveling through Europe again and again in the following years, I met so many people and have found lots of members of my Soul family and connected friendships. If I would try to talk about all the miracles that happened and of the people who recognized me from the Astral, my experiences with children and animals – this book could never be finished.

I am thankful to the Masters, angels and my closest friends, including all my friends and helpers on Earth for their love and support. They have given me the opportunity to share my life as a spiritual teacher, complete my mission and touch so many people's lives, more than I ever thought possible.

I enjoy every moment of my life with the certainty that I am always guided the right way and that I head into my future feeling positive and knowing it shall be an adventure of inspiration.

Amual Abactu Baraka Bashad
(May the universal love and blessings be)

Omnec

Image 19: First public appearence in Germany at a UFO Conference in Düsseldorf, 1992.

Image 20: Autographing her first book in Germany.

Image 21: With workshop group at the Mother Earth Center in Germany.

Image 22: With workshop-group in Switzerland, 1994.

Image 23: With Anja Schäfer at a Venus Dance Workshop, 1999.

Image 24: The "Dance of the Universe".

Image 25: Omnec with her sons Zandar and Jason.

Image 26: Omnec with her son Joe, 2007.

Image 27: In Missouri, 2007.

Image 28: In the flowers, 2000.

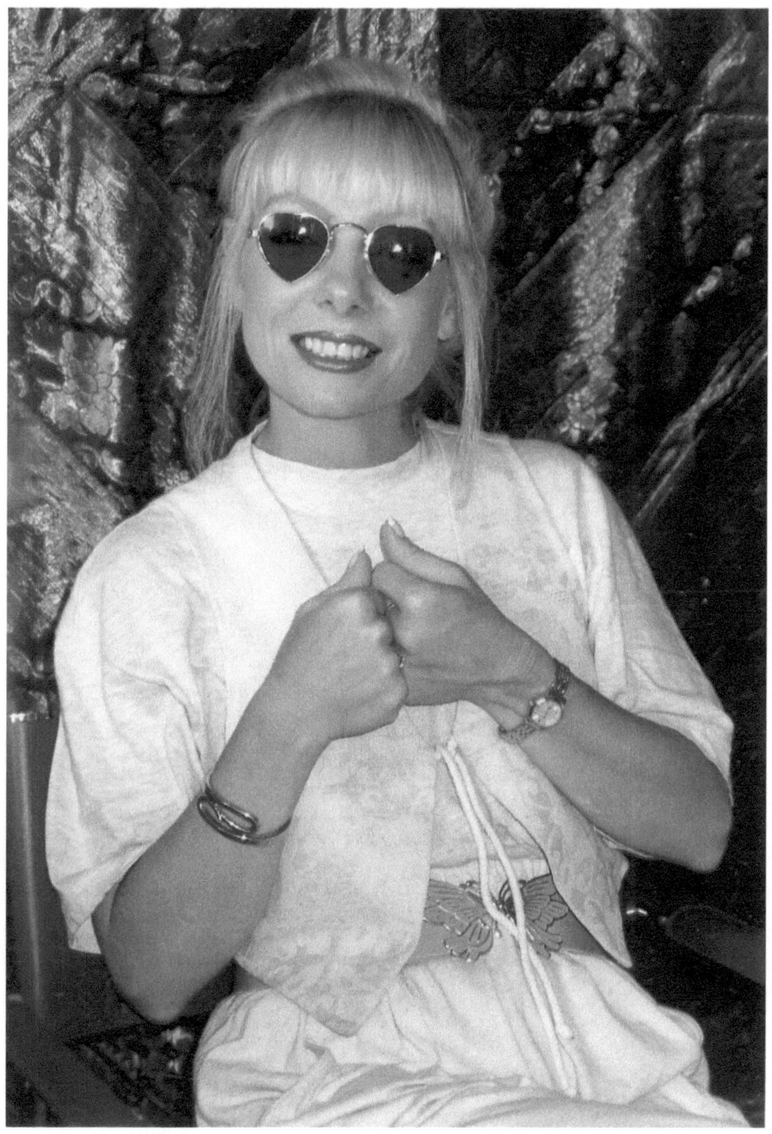

Image 29: A beautiful woman and beautiful Soul with a big heart.

Biographical Data

1948	(according to Earth calendar) born on the astral level of Venus
1955	Journey to Earth and stay in Agam Des, Tibet
1956	Journey from Tibet to Tennessee to grandmother of Sheila
1962	Journey to Sanibel Island, Florida to Donna and C.L.
1963	First rape through C.L.
1964	Move to Chicago
1965	Rape through Pedro
1966	Birth of JoJo
1967	Living together with Stan
1968	Birth of Tobi
1969	Encounter with Eckankar and Paul Twitchell; Manuscript "From Venus I Came" develops
1971	Birth of Zandar
1974	Attack of Pedro; loss of twins, heavy disease
1975	Separation from Stan
1977	Marriage with Bud, Birth of Jason
1984	Divorce from Bud
1986	Living together with Emanuel
1991	"From Venus I Came" is published in the USA; first public appearance at UFO-congress in Tuscon, Arizona
1992	First public appearance at a UFO-congress in Germany; first workshop
1993	Appearance in the well-known Jerry Springer Show (TV) together with JoJo, Tobi and Zandar

1994	"From Venus I Came" is published in Germany, first tour through Europe
1996	Death of Donna
1997	Encounter with Anja Schäfer, "German daughter" and Soul friend, beginning of cooperation
1998	CD "Message from Venus"
2000	CD "From Venus with Love", books "Angels Don't Cry", and "Handbook of Venusian Spirituality" (first releases in German only)
2009	Stroke and beginning of retirement
2011	Re-release of all books in German as a trilogy; promotion tour in Europe
2012	First release of all books in English as a compilation edition "The Venusian Trilogy"
2015	Appearance at the Mount Shasta Summer Conference, organized by Robert Potter
2018	Appearance at the Mount Shasta Summer Conference, encounter with Dr. Raymond Keller "Cosmic Ray", the Historian of the Venusians
2023	Re-release of all of Omnec's books in English and German
2023	Appearance at the Mount Shasta Summer Conference together with Dr. Raymond Keller and Anja Schäfer, part of the "Venus Ground Crew"

Image Directory

Publisher's Recommendations

Venus Pearls

From Venus I Came

Omnec Onec

Omnec Onec was born on the astral level of the planet Venus and came to Earth with her own physical body in 1955. She tells about the history, spirituality and culture of the Venusians, who once were a physical society and who have lived on the astral plane for a long time. Omnec tells about her first years of life on the astral Venus, explains why and how she came to Earth and what mission she has to fulfill here. This book is a unique document of its kind about the fabulous world of the astral. Being a sister planet to Earth, Venus has already gone through a similar process of transformation into a higher frequency plane as the Earth and its inhabitants are currently going through.

The history of Venus, delivered through Omnec Onec, along with its spiritual teachings, are a gift of pure love and show how the transformation into an expanded consciousness can be mastered in accordance with the universal laws of the Supreme Deity. This book is the authorized re-publication of the original version as written by Omnec Onec in the 1960s and first published in the USA in 1991 under the title UFO – From Venus I Came.

New Release 2023, DISCUS Publishing
ISBN: 978-3-910804-09-8

Angels Don't Cry
Omnec Onec
Angels Don't Cry is the stunning sequel to Omnec Onec's autobiography "**From Venus I Came**". This book is about the earthly life of the Venusian. Difficult family circumstances, constant changes of location and a spiritually unawakened environment presented very challenging conditions for the conscious child from Venus. The telepathic and sometimes physical contact with her friends and relatives from Venus as well as the awareness of her mission gave Omnec the strength to endure this life and to master it in love. Slowly, Omnec's way to the public was paved and the fulfillment of her mission as an Ambassador of Venus took hold with the first publication of her life story by Lt. Col. Ret. Wendelle C. Stevens in 1991.
New Release 2023, DISCUS Publishing
ISBN: 978-3-910804-10-4

Handbook of Venusian Spirituality
Omnec Onec
Essence of Spiritual Teachings
The truth is always simple. Practical and current, Omnec writes about the essence of creation, Soul, and life. This volume contains the essential message of the Venusian and gives practical keys for the expansion of consciousness.
Publisher's Note: This Handbook has never been published in English in this version as a separate book before. Parts of it are included in the Venusian Trilogy.
New Release 2023, DISCUS Publishing
ISBN: 978-3-910804-11-1

The Venusian Trilogy
Contents:
"From Venus I Came" - Autobiography Part 1
A classic in spiritual literature: In her autobiography, Omnec Onec portrays her ***life on the astral level of Venus*** and teaches ***timeless wisdom***. She speaks about the adventure of how and why she decided to manifest a physical body, and about her journey to Earth in 1955. This book was first published by the US Col. Wendelle C. Stevens in 1991.
"Angels Don't Cry" - Autobiography Part 2
In the continuation of her autobiography, Omnec tells her experiences on Earth.
"My Message" - Essence of spiritual teachings. Omnec writes about the essence of creation, Soul, and life. This part also contains a chapter about the evolution of Souls on Earth.
Note: This edition contains all of Omnec's three books and was compiled and in some parts revised by her supporter and deceased previous publisher Kouki Wohlwend in 2012.
544 pages with colored pictures
ISBN: 978-3-9523815-2-6

Simply Wisdom and Love - Venusian Spirituality
Omnec Onec and Anja Schäfer
The world as we know it is changing rapidly, the Transformation Process of the Earth is in progress. The current world system, in which a few powerful people control and manipulate others, is coming to an end. The Earth is ascending to a higher frequency. Thanks to courageous messengers such as Omnec Onec, we are reminded of what we have long forgotten:

that our ancestors came from other star systems and galaxies. Our existence is not limited to the physical life we live. We are all Souls and universal beings, created by a loving Creator.
Contents: The Unknown History of our Solar System and the ongoing Transformation of the Earth from Venusian perspective · "The True Story of Christ" · "A Venusian Letter" · Transcripts of Omnec's public appearances with Q&A · Project Omnec's Oasis – a Place to live in Harmony with the Universe
Loving, wise, inspiring. This book is a light focus for the expansion of consciousness and gives a deep insight into the teachings of the Venusians.
DISCUS Publishing, 2016
ISBN: 978-3-9817441-0-1

Venus and I
Anja Schäfer
My Journey of Coming to Remembrance of my Soul Mission
— 25 years with Omnec Onec —
A Story about Initiations, the Transformation of the Earth, and Love
"This book describes the author's spiritual awakening process. Her refreshing and witty way of writing made me feel like I was along on her journey."
Axel
Contents: Venus Ambassadors, Omnec Onec, Phaistos Disc, Atlantis, Cyclic time – Linear time, Venus-Germany-Connection, Transformation, Ascension, Awakening, Earth's future, Artificial timeline and Natural timeline, Spiritual Practices, Levels of Consciousness, Twin Flames, Jo Conrad Interview with Omnec Onec.
"I am certain today that I have incarnated as one of the souls to break down encrusted structures and to help both myself and people to allow true, divine love to rise and to embody. We are here to help Mother Earth to ascend to a higher vibrational fre-

quency and to end the age of darkness and ignorance."
Anja Schäfer – *venus-spirit.com*
New Release 2023, DISCUS Publishing
ISBN: 978-3-910804-02-9

Venus Historian Dr. Raymond Keller

Dr. Raymond Andrew Keller aka "Cosmic Ray" is the Historian of the Venusians, contactee, UFO researcher, author and retired Doctor of History. Ray's VENUS RISING book series explores numerous facets of Venus. Well documented and based on personal research and years of experience, Ray's books reveal amazing connections from the perspectives of history, mythology, theosophy, space exploration, ufology, contactees, Venusians, spirituality, and current events.

Venus Rising – A Concise History of the Second Planet, 2016
The Final Countdown: Rockets to Venus, 2018
Cosmic Rays Excellent Venus Adventure, 2018
The Vast Venus Conspiracy, 2021
Lady Columba Venus Revelations, 2021
Flying Saucers and the Venus Legacy, 2022

From Venus They Come, 2022
Book 1 to 7 published by Headline Books, WV, USA ***https://headlinebooks.com/*** in cooperation with Dr. Keller.
More about Cosmic Ray: ***https://venus-spirit.com/ray***

The Gospels of Thomas and Mary Magdalene
Dr. Raymond Keller
This Gospel of Thomas, inclusive of the Gospel of Mary Magdalene, was found at the Nag Hammadi site in the Egyptian desert in December of 1945 along with some other books collectively called the "Nag Hammadi Library." These texts were very fragmented with age and in a state of advanced decay. The original parchments now rest in the Coptic Museum in Cairo. They have been thought to have been written and dated from 100-245 A.D., according to some sources.

Until today these sacred texts have only been able to be partially interpreted by scholars because no complete record of these texts has ever been found. That these texts are even real is debated by many. It is possible, but doubtful, that these texts are in their complete form anywhere in the world, not even in the library beneath the Vatican. Even if these texts were there, they could not be as complete or as accurate as this version for this edition is a supernatural gift to the faithful through the Hierarchy of Light.
2022, DISCUS Publishing
ISBN: 978-3-9817441-9-4

CDs from Omnec Onec

In collaboration with the music producer Wulf Wemmje, Omnec Onec created these three beautiful CDs under Venusian inspiration.

Soul Journey

Guided Meditation with various music compositions corresponding to the levels of consciousness. Mantras and visualizations support the experience of the different dimensions from the physical through the astral, the causal, and the etheric dimension to the God planes. *"The Soul Travel technique enables you to leave the physical body withouth the connection of the silver chord. You travel with light and sound and have access to any dimension you wish, where you can gain knowledge or make an experience for the benefit of Soul while still existing in the physical."*

My Mission on Earth

Omnec tells the story of her origin and shares universal knowledge

Listen to Omnec's fascinating voice, embedded in sound spheres and Venusian inspired music, how she describes in her own words the connection of Venus to the history of the Earth and the purpose and goal of her adventurous transfer from the astral plane to the physical Earth.

From Venus with Love

Omnec speaks and sings about love with spherical background music. "Love in the physical realm is one of the most powerful emotions, that is expressed in unlimited ways. Love can overwhelm the senses, or love can be subtle. Love is different for each of us. Love can be used to create, or love can destroy. Love can be used to manipulate and control, or love can be given freely. Love can make you a prisoner, and love can make you free. Once you have experienced love in all forms, then you get to know unconditional love. Venus Love is unconditional love." (Omnec Onec, Introduction CD "From Venus with Love")

The CDs are available physically and as downloads in our **Venus Spirit Online-Shop https://venus-spirit.com. Here,** you can also enjoy audio samples.

Contact

Anja Schäfer

Venus Spirit Website: ***https://venus-spirit.com***
Omnec Onec Website: ***https://omnec-onec.com***

Venus Spirit YouTube Channel:
https://www.youtube.com/@venus-spirit

Please subscribe to our **Venus Spirit Newsletter.**

Let's connect more and more with each other and create an amazing new Earth together!

May the Universal Love and Blessings Be

Anja ♥

www.ingramcontent.com/pod-product-compliance
Ingram Content Group UK Ltd.
Pitfield, Milton Keynes, MK11 3LW, UK
UKHW041838190726
13854UKWH00002B/603